FROM THE ABUNDANCE
OF THE HEART

FROM THE ABUNDANCE OF THE HEART

CATHOLIC EVANGELISM FOR ALL CHRISTIANS

Stephen Cottrell

DARTON · LONGMAN + TODD

To the priests, people and parishes
of the Reading Episcopal Area.

First published in 2006 by
Darton, Longman and Todd Ltd
1 Spencer Court
140–142 Wandsworth High Street
London SW18 4JJ

Reprinted 2007 and 2009

ISBN 10: 0–232–52636–2
ISBN 13: 978–0–232–52636–3

A catalogue record for this book is available from the British Library.

Unless otherwise stated, the Scripture quotations in this publication
are taken from the New Revised Standard Version © 1989, 1995. Division
of Christian Education of the National Council of the Churches of Christ
in the United States of America.

Designed and produced by Sandie Boccacci
Phototypeset in 9.75pt/11.75pt Times New Roman
Printed and bound in Great Britain by
Intype Libra Ltd, London

'It is out of the abundance of the heart that the mouth speaks.'

Luke 6:45

Anyone who reads in the New Testament the origins of the Church, follows her history step by step and watches her live and act, sees that she is linked to evangelisation in her most intimate being.

The Church is born of the evangelising activity of Jesus and the Twelve. She is the normal, desired, most immediate and most visible fruit of this activity: 'Go, therefore, make disciples of all the nations' (Matthew 28.19). Now, 'they accepted what he said and were baptised. That very day about three thousand were added to their number ... Day by day the Lord added to their community those destined to be saved' (Acts 2.41 & 47).

Having been born consequently out of being sent, the Church in turn is sent by Jesus. The Church remains in the world when the Lord of glory returns to the father. She remains as a sign – simultaneously obscure and luminous – of a new presence of Jesus, of his departure and of his permanent presence. She prolongs and continues him. And it is above all his mission and his condition of being an evangeliser that she is called upon to continue. For the Christian community is never closed in upon itself. The intimate life of this community – the life of listening to the Word and the Apostles' teaching, charity lived in a fraternal way, the sharing of bread – this intimate life only acquires its full meaning when it becomes witness, when it evokes admiration and conversion and becomes the preaching and proclamation of the Good News. Thus it is that the whole Church receives the mission to evangelise, and the work of each individual member is important for the whole.

Evangelii Nuntiandi[1]

CONTENTS

ACKNOWLEDGEMENTS

For many years it seemed that if anyone in the Church of England was planning a conference or training event on mission and needed to provide the all-important balance between speakers of different church traditions my name was on the usual list of Anglo-Catholic suspects. Indeed, for nearly ten years the main focus of my ministry was as Diocesan Missioner in the Diocese of Wakefield and then as Missioner with Springboard, the initiative in evangelism of the Archbishops of Canterbury and York. I have spent a lot of time trying to support and encourage others in a way of evangelising that can fit in with the ethos and spirituality of churches of a catholic tradition.

There is much work to be done in this area. I look back to my own training at St Stephen's House and realise that although I learnt a lot of good things, evangelism wasn't really one of them. Yet here we are in a missionary situation and needing to develop a ministry of evangelism within the local church community. Thankfully, there are signs of hope around. The quite recently formed Society of Catholic Priests declares catholic evangelism to be one of its twin aims. Both Forward in Faith and Affirming Catholicism recognise the importance of communicating and sharing Christian faith. We no longer seem to argue about whether we should be doing evangelism, just how. Churches of all traditions recognise and welcome the particular emphases of a catholic approach and are open to learn. And there are more priests on the list of conference speakers!

This book is offered as a contribution to this growing awareness of the importance of evangelism. It is written with catholic parishes in mind but is offered to all churches that want to develop an evangelistic ministry and think there is something to be learned from an approach which is informed by catholic spirituality and practice. For me, personally, it represents the fruits of about ten years' thinking and praying and doing evangelism up and down the country.

In particular this book began life nearly ten years ago as a much smaller booklet published by DLT and Affirming Catholicism and simply called *Catholic Evangelism*. Those of you who read that book will recognise parts of this book. But this is much more than a re-issue. *From the Abundance of the Heart* is about four times the length and tries to give a clear theological rationale for the ministry of evangelism as well as a much more thorough-going guide on how to do it.

That book was commissioned and edited by Fr Jeffrey John. I am thankful to him for the opportunity he gave me to get writing about evangelism. Now, for other reasons, our two names are inextricably linked, but this book gives me a small way of acknowledging my debt to him, along with many others who have taught and encouraged me in the ministry of evangelism, among them: Archbishop David Hope and Bishop David Thomas, who were my Principals at Theological College; Fr Michael Hart, who when I was first ordained showed me what it could mean to be a missionary priest; Bishop Michael Marshall and Bishop Lindsay Urwin, who are both catholic evangelists; Canon Martin Warner who has always encouraged me in my calling to mission; and three evangelical priests from whom I have learned so much Steven Croft, Robert Warren and James Lawrence.

I was invited to write the book by Brendan Walsh at DLT just before I was asked to become a bishop. I really wondered whether I could justify the time required in what has become a rather unrelenting schedule. I therefore also want to record my thanks to Sheila Watson, Archdeacon of Buckingham, for her great encouragement that I should not feel guilty about setting aside time to write. And it is for this reason, more than any other, that I dedicate the book to the priests and people of the Reading Episcopal Area. Many of the parishes in this area are of a central or catholic tradition. As I have written I have held these parishes in my prayers. This book is my way of laying before them a vision for an evangelising church and a way of getting started in this ministry. And even for those churches who would not call themselves catholic I hope there may be insights and observations here that will encourage and help them in their outreach. As I have said in many sermons already: our task is to proclaim the faith afresh and to make Christ known. These challenges from the Declaration of Assent are set before us whenever a priest is licensed to a parish. They should be motivation enough for the task that lies ahead.

I also wish to record thanks to my colleagues Norman Russell, Archdeacon of Berkshire, Janet Russell, Parish Development Adviser for this Episcopal Area, Jane Cooper, my PA, and Lesley Young, my Secretary. In their different ways all of them have supported me through the first year of my episcopal ministry and enabled me to write this book.

STEPHEN COTTRELL
Michaelmass, 2005

INTRODUCTION: DEFINING TERMS

THE WORD **MISSION** DOESN'T APPEAR in the Bible. It is a word the church uses, usually to describe its own work and ministry. But instead of talking about 'the mission of the church' – a phrase which trips easily off the tongue – it would be much better to talk about 'the mission of God'. The daring revelation of the Christian faith is that God has a mission. The story of the Bible is the story of a God who is concerned with the world. So concerned that God enters the world in order to reveal its true beauty and bring it to fulfilment. This is the purpose of God and it is a purpose that encompasses every aspect of the creation.

God is concerned for the welfare and well-being of the planet, for the pursuit of justice, and for the salvation (which means the healing and restoration) of every individual human being. God's mission is vast and beautiful. God is the missionary.

THE GOD WHO SENDS

A word that is used in the Bible is **sending**.[1] God acts in and through the creation he has made. First of all God chooses and commissions a people through whom his love and purposes are made known. Finally, called from among this people, God sends his son into the world. Jesus is the one who makes God known. Jesus comes to fulfil God's purposes and reveal God's love. He is the 'image of the invisible God' (Colossians 1:15). Through him we have access to God (see Ephesians 2:18). In one startling phrase Jesus is actually called 'apostle' which means 'the one who is sent' (Hebrews 3:1).

After his death and resurrection Jesus' own mission continues through the ministry of the **Spirit**. The presence of the Spirit is the presence of Jesus, reminding the church of the truth that Jesus taught (John 14:26) but also guiding into all truth. In this sense his ascension is not about departure but signals an arrival and a new age where God is intimately available at all times and in all places through the sending of the Spirit. 'It is to your advantage that I go away,' says Jesus in St John's Gospel, 'for if I do not go away, the Advocate will not come to you; but if I go, I will send him to you' (John 16:7).

In the Creed, of course, the word **apostolic** is used to describe the church. When we say the church is apostolic we are saying the church is sent – sent by Jesus to participate in the work of God. In other words, God's purposes revealed in Christ are now being worked out in the hearts and minds of human beings through the indwelling, cajoling and perfecting of the Holy Spirit. The mission of God, revealed in Christ, is entrusted to the church. But it is still God's mission. And we can still find God at work in many places outside of the church.

As for the **church** itself, it only makes sense as we perceive ourselves as the community of those who are called together and sent out by Christ. Through Christ we are called into community with God; through Christ we are sent out to share God's mission in the world. All this is summed up in two phrases of Jesus that we find in John's Gospel. On the night before he dies, giving his disciples the new commandment that they must love one another and love the world with the same self-forgetful love with which he has loved them, he says: 'As the Father has loved me, so I have loved you' (John 15:9). On the evening of the first Easter day, finding them frightened, confused and locked away he arrives in their presence and says, 'As the Father has sent me, so I send you' (John 20:21). Thus the Christ who is sent by God is the one who sends and commissions the church. We place ourselves in the sending flow of God's love. It is significant for John's Gospel that this sending of the infant church is also the Pentecost moment when the Spirit is sent, for without the Spirit this mission cannot happen.

We are the 'gathered in and the sent out' community: the church that is loved by God and sent by God. Our mission should be indistinguishable from God's mission (though this is rarely the case, we are so preoccupied by secondary matters). In this respect a good definition of mission would be: 'seek to discern God's purposes for the world; roll up your sleeves and join in!'

This book is about **evangelism**. Evangelism is that aspect of mission which brings people to faith in Christ. It is the process whereby people become disciples of Christ. It is still the work of God. The Holy Spirit is the Evangelist. The Holy Spirit is the one who is sent to enable us to participate in God's mission. As the Roman Catholic documents on evangelisation make clear: 'The Holy Spirit is the principle agent of evangelisation; it is he who impels each individual to proclaim the gospel and it is he who in the depths of consciences causes the words of salvation to be accepted and understood.'[2] Hence, the awakening of faith in an individual is not something that can be engineered by human endeavour or persuasion. All our programmes, techniques and strategies are nothing without the gentle action of the Spirit.

We are standing on holy ground. The individual human response to the call and commission of God is always a profound mystery. In everything that we do, and despite appearances to the contrary, the Holy Spirit broods over the creation bringing order, beauty and joy.

Neither can the work of evangelism be separated from the whole of God's mission, since the Christian vocation to live in community with God must always include doing the work of God and working for God's purposes. This is why the great commission at the end of Matthew's Gospel asks us to 'make disciples' (28:19). A disciple is one who follows the call of Christ. However, in the New Testament the twelve who are called disciples – ones who follow – are also called apostles – ones who are sent. This dynamic life of being called to follow and commissioned to be sent out, continues to this day. It is the work of the Spirit.

It is also impossible to write a book about evangelism without saying something about the *evangelion* – the good news – that is the root meaning of the word itself. However, as John Finney reminds us, the New Testament also uses the word *mysterion* to describe the gospel of Christ.[3] Christians from a catholic tradition have always been at ease with this way of approaching the gospel. Our evangelism has often been rooted in very practical social action and the beauty of worship that would draw people into the presence of God. This was certainly the instinctive strategy of that great generation of priests who planted churches in some of the poorest slums of Victorian England and for whom presence and proclamation went hand in hand.

Later in the book we will think about the gospel as a multi-faceted jewel, something that cannot be reduced to a single phrase, still less a slogan. But if you forced me into a corner and said that I must come up with a soundbite for the gospel, then I would say this: 'The good news for today is that in Christ we can become ourselves. Because of what God has done in Christ we can become the people and the world we are meant to be.' It is a new way of being human that God has shown us and made possible for us in the life, death and resurrection of Jesus. Helping people to receive and embrace this new humanity so that our lives and our world reflect the beauty of God is the ministry of evangelism, but it is as much about living the mysterious beauty of this gospel as it is proclaiming it. Nevertheless this book is designed to be a practical guide to the ministry of evangelism. It will be about how we actually *do* it, participating with God in his longing to enjoy community with every human being. But it is important to be clear about the words that are being used and what they mean since these words are very often used in different ways.

To many the word evangelism still conjures up negative images of coercion and manipulation. It is still the case that many Christians evangelise in ways that seem far removed from the joy and generosity that characterised the life of Christ. What we are called to share is the abundant life that is shown us in Christ. The *way* we do this will be as important as whether we do it.

MOTIVATION FOR EVANGELISM

This leads us on to ask about our motivation for evangelism. I well remember visiting a church in a very wealthy part of the country. I was there to speak about evangelism. After the service someone came and patted me on the back and thanked me for what I'd said. 'Of course, we don't need to worry about evangelism', he added. 'Our church is full on Sunday and we pay the quota!' Sadly, his attitude is all too prevalent. But if our motivation for evangelism is filling the pews or paying the share we will not get very far. This kind of desperation will be spotted easily by those we might target. If it is spiritual truth they are after they will know to look elsewhere.

Neither can geting people into heaven, or saving people from hell be our motivation for evangelism. The new relationship we have with God in Christ and, therefore, the life of heaven, is freely available to everyone. Because this is supremely about God's love, then it cannot be forced upon us. God freely offers it to all, and we freely decide whether to receive it or not. The consistent message of the New Testament is that we will be surprised in heaven, finding those we considered last to be ahead of us. In other words – and it needs saying over and over again – judgement is God's department. And the one he has appointed judge is the same one who knows our frailty and our failings better than we know them ourselves and in him mercy and justice have embraced. We must go further: at the heart of our message is not that we are condemned but acquitted. Everyone has been let off by God's work in Christ. Robert Farrar Capon, in his delightfully entitled book *The Mystery of Christ and why we don't get it,* describes it in this provocative way:

> In Jesus' death and resurrection, the whole test-passing, brownie-point-earning rigmarole of the human race has been cancelled for lack of interest on God's part ... all we have to do is trust his assurance that losers are his cup of tea.[4]

He goes on:

> If the gospel is proclaimed correctly it is always going to sound nuts. As a matter of fact, it will always sound wrong, and immoral, and threatening to all the values we know and love even though they're killing us.[5]

'There is therefore now no condemnation for those who are in Christ Jesus' (Romans 8:1) is the summarising statement of Paul's radical and unrelenting conviction that in Christ we are set free from the false values and withering judgements with which we continue to measure, define and exclude each other. 'While we still were sinners' – i.e. before we confessed our penitence or even knew Christ – 'Christ died for us' (Romans 5:8). Therefore it cannot be our holiness, or goodness, or even our penitence that puts us right with God. No, nothing we do can put us right with God and earn salvation. Only what God has done can make a difference, and in Christ God has already made all the difference. This is something we can only receive, never earn. And on that day when all of us – whatever our faith or lack of it – see God face to face, if we still refuse to receive it, then we choose separation, and this is hell. But for the time being and, in our sharing of God's mission here on earth, saving lost souls from hell can never, of itself, be our motivation. Rather it must be the offering of the gift.

And the gift – the precious mystery of faith – cannot be reduced or contained. It is in relationship with God that we discover this new way of being human. Because it is the multi-faceted jewel of a gospel, then even those who are closest to the ways of God will still not see it all. (The Holy Spirit leads us into truth.) Therefore we might say that the highest motivation for evangelism is a longing to see the whole picture, even though we know that in this life we never will. But we so thirst for the beauty and goodness of God that we long to see the world as God sees it and we long to see people as God sees them.

I would sum this up in two words – justice and joy. First of all justice. We long to see the world ordered, sustained and flourishing in the way that God intends. Therefore our evangelism is linked with our mission. Although they are not the same thing and, as we saw earlier, it is helpful to be clear about the differences between the two – mission being concerned with all God's purposes in the world, evangelism with helping people to become disciples – there is a link between them because the one who is called is also the one who is sent. It is only by shaping the minds, hearts and wills of all people that we shall find the peace and stability for our world which is God's purpose. This is the big picture in which the ministry of evangelism – a ministry in which all Christian people share – contributes and energises the church to participate more fully in God's mission in the world. It also prevents the gospel being put into a compartment. It is not service *or* evangelism. It must always be both.

And this is why when people say evangelism is not about bums on seats I always want to say, 'Yes, it is.' Because it is about people. It is about the gift of a re-ordered creation being made available to everyone. It is about the big picture of our participation in God's life and mission. For bums on seats read hands ready to serve, ears to listen, hearts to love and minds shaped by the will and purpose of God. Without people there will be no mission. Moreover, I am yet to meet a priest who doesn't know exactly how many people attended church the previous Sunday. We care about numbers because we care about people. We want the church to grow: not because we are concerned with building the earthly empire of the church, but because we want to build God's kingdom in the world.

And it is about joy. As we shall explore in the next chapter with regard to the link between evangelism and spirituality, we give from the overflow of what we have received. We glimpse the beauty of God; we learn what he has done for us in Christ; we respond to his call in our life; and we discover a new joy and a new purpose. It overwhelms us and it completes us. We find a new humanity and a new love for life. We become the people we are meant to be and the joy that it is within overflows into every other aspect of our life. We have no choice: the life we live sings out of the faith we share. Or at least it should … We will return to this subject!

THE ACCOMPANIED JOURNEY

Evangelism can provide a cutting edge to mission. Without a specifically evangelistic ministry there is always a danger that our mission ceases to be specifically Christian.

Evangelism is a distinctive ministry. Although it is true that all Christian ministry is evangelistic (in the sense that it has the potential to reveal or obscure the purposes of God), we need to identify an appropriately specific way of making God's love known – of offering the gift – so that people will want to respond and participate in God's purposes and become disciples themselves.

For most people today becoming a Christian will be like a journey. The concept of pilgrimage and accompanied journey is central to this book. The ministry of evangelism is about helping people make the journey. Although this journey will take many forms, we need to develop particular attitudes, activities and ministries within the church if we are going to be faithful to our calling to make disciples. We will explore these in detail. It is this particular and distinctive ministry, and what it will look like in the life of the local church and in the given circumstances of our own culture close to the beginning of a new century, that is the subject of this book.

Finally this book is concerned with 'catholic evangelism'. In one sense there is no such thing. There is just the ministry of evangelism which belongs to the whole Church, and then the particular and distinctive ways that different Christians go about it according to the instincts and insights of their own tradition. For Christians of a catholic tradition this will mean:

- an emphasis on the interior life and the attraction and beauty of holiness
- a belief in the converting power of worship, especially sacramental worship
- an understanding of the ministry of evangelism as accompanying people on a journey into the fullness of life
- a passionate concern for justice
- a conviction that coming to Christ also means becoming part of the church.

These insights are not, of course, exclusive to catholic Christianity. The word 'catholic' does not just describe a strand within the Christian Church, but, enshrined in the Creed, describes a fundamental aspect of our life together, whatever our tradition. These are the distinctive things that shape catholic spirituality and therefore shape the ways catholic Christians approach evangelism. Therefore, this book, which is written primarily to encourage Christians of a catholic tradition to be more confident and purposeful in their own evangelism, is also offered as good news for all Christians so that we can work together to bring God's kingdom to the world. We have much to learn from each other.

We can sum up the terms that are used in this book in this way:

Mission – 'everything that God's love revealed in Christ sends to the world. It embraces the pursuit of justice and peace and the care of creation, as well as the sharing of faith.'[6]

Evangelism – that aspect of mission which is concerned with bringing people to faith in Christ: the process whereby people become disciples of Christ. It cannot be separated from the whole of God's mission, but for the purposes of this book will be dealt with on its own.

Disciple/apostle – someone who participates in God's purposes for the world. Hence the missionary church seeks to live and share the gospel in such a way that others join in Christian community, and dedicate their lives to God's mission in the world.

These definitions echo the five marks of mission developed by the Anglican Consultative Council. They are :

1. to proclaim the good news of the kingdom
2. to teach, baptise and nurture new believers
3. to respond to human need by loving service

4. to seek to transform the unjust structures of society
5. to strive to safeguard the integrity of creation and sustain and renew the life of the earth.

The first two marks are clearly concerned with evangelism. But we are discovering afresh that responding to human need and working to transform society is one of the best ways of doing it. Good in itself, because it is a participation in God's mission, but also good in commending to others the ways of God.

It is this understanding of evangelism as making disciples, and seeing participation in God's mission as the authentic sign of a disciple's life, that I want to emphasise.

Part One of the book is more theoretical, exploring God's vision for this sort of evangelising church. Part Two is more practical, looking at how we develop the structures and ministries that will establish the ministry of evangelism in the local church so that we will see people coming to faith.

The book also has a story running through it of how one church went about developing a ministry of evangelism. Although this is a fictitious story, it is loosely based upon a parish I know and have worked with. But as soon as one starts telling a particular story of a particular place it is easy for others to dismiss it, because it is unlike the context in which they are working. So please, don't be put off. The story tells you what *can* happen, not what *will* happen. Making the ministry of evangelism your own is your story. A story already begun and a story waiting to be continued. And it will be fruitful in different ways according to your different contexts. The important thing is to get started.

PART ONE

GOD'S VISION FOR AN EVANGELISING CHURCH

OR
WHOSE CHURCH IS IT ANYWAY?

I

PRAYER – THE WAY WE ACCESS AND ARE RENEWED BY GOD'S VISION

FOR NEARLY TEN YEARS much of my ministry was involved in helping churches engage with the ministry of evangelism. On many occasions I would go to a church to talk about evangelism and sit down with their PCC or another group within the parish, and after about ten minutes I would shut up about evangelism and start talking about prayer instead.

To put it bluntly: you can't give what you haven't got. How stupid of us to think that we could ever be effective in evangelism unless it arose from an authentic and lived spirituality.

The most basic meaning of the word 'evangelism' is the sharing of good news. Although many people in the church today are still suspicious about evangelism, the sharing of good news is something we do all the time. If we have experienced something as good and joyful, there is nothing more natural than to share it with others. So, if we go to a good film, read a good book, if our football team wins, or if a new child is born into our family, we tell people about it. We don't feel we are oppressing them in any way by telling them about it. We don't necessarily expect, and we certainly don't demand, that they see the film, read the book, support the team or adopt the baby! We are not looking for any reward. We simply share our excitement with them. We have experienced something to be good. We tell people about it. We can do no other.

Therefore, before going any further, any church that wants to develop a ministry of evangelism needs to ask itself: 'Do we experience the Christian faith and our membership of the church as good news for our own lives? Is it actually shaping and informing our life in such a way that we could ever imagine telling anyone anything about it?' And if the answer is no – if we actually experience the church as dull, life denying, tired, pointless; if the life we lead on Monday is completely disconnected from the faith we celebrate on Sunday – then it is little wonder that not much evangelism happens. There is no good news to share. Or else the good news is entirely an abstract, second-hand set of propositions about God and the universe. We may believe the Christian faith to be true (though this may also be the problem) but it is not true in any way that is remotely relevant to life.

The thinking about evangelism that shapes this book is that we give from the overflow of what we have received. Therefore a way of moving on from the question 'Do we experience the Christian faith as good news?' is 'Are we in a place of receiving where the goodness of what God reveals to us in Christ can actually start shaping and changing our lives?' And what would such a place look like? In other words, are we developing in our churches an authentic and lived spirituality that can shape the lives of individuals and communities? Before the church can evangelise the world, the gospel must evangelise the church.

And here we come to the first of many paradoxes that inevitably shape any consideration of Christian faith. It is in giving that we receive. We may not get very far in enabling the gospel to evangelise the church if we do it in a vacuum, locked away inside church buildings and church culture. It might best be done in the community around us. After all, the *raison d'être* of the church is the needs of the world. With proper humility we need to allow the questions of the world to shape the agenda of the church.

We also need a keen awareness that whenever we dare to speak of God, and whenever we deal with the deepest mysteries of the human response to God, and the issues of life and death that go with it, we are treading on sacred ground. It is not something over which we have authority or control. Aware of our own shortcomings and needs, the best way to proceed is to recognise ourselves as fellow seekers in the way of faith. You can't accompany anyone from a seated position!

In other words we get on with the ministry of evangelism, but stop doing it in a way that suggests we have all the answers (Jesus is the answer. Now, what was the question?). Too often what passes for evangelism in the church is really just a parading of slogans or, worse, a condemnation of anyone who doesn't share our world view.

Someone has defined evangelism as one beggar telling another beggar where to get bread. Rather than being paralysed by the recognition that our own lives are only very dimly lit by the gospel, we could use this as a starting point for activities that help us address questions of meaning and faith in a way that will allow us to make common cause with others – as yet outside the Christian community – who are asking similar questions.

We will return to this approach when we consider the actual doing of evangelism later in the book. For the time being it is important to be clear about this most basic realisation: the chief reason that many churches struggle with evangelism – and so much more – is that they are not places of prayer. Addressing this issue must be the first step towards becoming an evangelising, mission-shaped church. This is the way we will grow in our own relationship with God. This is the way we will find a faith to share as well as a natural and unforced way of sharing it. This is the way we will discover God's vision for God's church. Joyfully – and with some relief – we embrace the paradox that the best way of helping the church discover an authentic spirituality might also be the best way of evangelising a spiritually starved culture. But this is another subject we will return to.

LEARNING TO PRAY

Jesus says, 'give and it will be given to you. A good measure, pressed down, shaken together, running over, will be put into your lap; for the measure you give will be the measure you get back' (Luke 6:38). This is undoubtedly true for the ministry of evangelism. If anyone says to me they would like to grow in their faith, then my best advice is to suggest they try and give their faith away. It is in facing the issues that are involved in living and sharing the faith that we are most likely to discover what we actually believe and what its relevance is (or isn't!) for our lives.

We will also learn to pray like never before. We will quickly discover that neither the example of our goodness nor the eloquence of our speech will ever make anyone into a Christian. But we will also discover another important gospel paradox. The humble admission of our failure, and the testimony of the grace and help we have received, will really communicate, and in giving we will have received.

Let us then return to the question of prayer. How shall we define prayer? Well, think of God as the great Lover who longs to communicate his love to his people. The Christian revelation is that God longs to enjoy community with the creation he has made and particularly with humankind. We are the people who are able to respond with the selfsame love from which we were created. Therefore God is constantly coming into our presence to proclaim his love. Supremely God has come to us through Jesus Christ whose own life is a perfect statement of God's intent. He comes to pledge his troth to us. His life is a demonstration of love. Through the outpouring of the Holy Spirit this same offer of love is made to the world today.

Moreover, we are the Beloved. We are the object of God's love. We are made in his image and alone in all creation (as far as our present understanding can tell) able to return the love we receive. Because it is love, God can never, and will never, force or coerce us into responding, but he always waits upon us. Through the indwelling of the Holy Spirit, when we do make the free response of love (more of this later) we are brought into community with God.

We could therefore define prayer as 'The Lover coming into the presence of the Beloved and saying "I love you".'[1] It describes not just the heart of prayer, but also the heart of faith, since the two must go together.

It also begins with God's initiative: his love for us and our openness to receive that love.

What we call prayer is actually our response to God. In its most raw and basic form, it is the longing of our heart to know God. In response to what we see and experience God doing for us in Christ – the showing forth of love – we splutter in reply, 'I love you too'.

This resonance in the human heart between the love of God and the response of the human spirit is in fact the highest form of prayer and will be the stuff of eternity. Helping people into this prayer requires that we preach the gospel. We tell people about the love of God in Christ and the affirmation, forgiveness and acceptance that it offers. We tell of our own need of God and of the change and blessing it has brought to our lives. It is not a formula or a technique – though in time formulas and techniques may help us grow in making an ordered response to God, for discipline as well as desire is required in the life of prayer. We gently lead people to a place where they can receive God's love. This happens in fleeting moments and in ordered occasions – in times of prayer, in fellowship with other people, and in the worship of the church. And we help people make their response, using the forms of the liturgy, or their own words, or the deep and expectant silence of contemplation. People learn to receive, and because what they receive is good and beautiful they can't help sharing it, they can't stop it making a difference in their lives.

As we shall see later, this doesn't mean that we don't need specific evangelism strategies and programmes. But it does mean that none of them will be any help whatsoever unless we have first become a people of prayer. When the church becomes a house of prayer, says Brother Roger of Taizé, people will come running. In my own ministry as a priest I have glimpsed the truth of this astonishing claim.

2

A THEOLOGICAL VISION:
THE FAITH THAT CHANGES OUR LIFE
AND THE GOSPEL WE SHARE

As WE PRAY, as we experience ourselves to be the Beloved of God, and as we know God to be the world's great Lover, so our own capacity for love is extended and expanded. We begin to love the world more, we begin to love each other more and we begin to catch hold of God's vision for God's church in God's world. We think less about our own plans and begin to wonder what God's purposes might be. Catching hold of this vision is what I am calling our participation in the mission of God: placing ourselves in the sending flow of God's love. It is through a life lived in community with God, a life shaped by intimate prayer and the worship of the church, that this happens. It could hardly be any other, since the Christian revelation of God is of a community of persons, whose pleasant company with each other is an ever-widening circle of love, endlessly creative, self-giving and inclusive. The God who is community wishes to extend the invitation of community to the whole creation and especially to every human person. Thus the proclamation of Christ is the proclamation of a person through whom we have community with God (see Ephesians 2:17). The Christian faith – or what we should properly call the Christian life – is an invitation to join this community. This is why, from a catholic perspective, the invitation to know Christ is always an invitation to community with God within the household of the church.

This abundant life is revealed in the life, death and resurrection of Jesus, but as we will explore in more detail when we discuss how we accompany people on the way to faith, it is best understood as a demonstration of God's own love, and an invitation to receive it for ourselves. Therefore the work of evangelism is much more than asking people to give intellectual assent to the truths about God – inviting them to believe certain things – it is a call to receive the generosity of God and then to live lives of generosity and hospitality that invite others in.

Although we shall deal with this in detail in the penultimate chapter, developing a generous and hospitable Christian community is in many respects a vital first step to becoming an evangelising church. But as we have already noted, this sort of growth and development is not linear or formulaic. It is not a matter of following certain steps, so much as living out certain attitudes and developing a certain kind of personhood in our relationship with each other and the world.

So we begin with prayer – our own relationship with God – and then we try to see the world and ourselves from God's perspective, and try to grow a Christian community which reflects these attitudes and values. This will be an authentic Christian community. It will also be an attractive community that people will want to join. However, it is not a matter of waiting to see who comes and then making them welcome. It must involve living out what we believe in a way that raises questions about the whole of life, and encourages others to explore.[1] It must also include ways of helping others to make the journey we are travelling.

Robert Warren has written powerfully about this approach to church life which emphasises health rather than growth. His book *Building Missionary Congregations* has helped many churches re-think their ministry from the perspective of mission. In turn, the research he did in many growing churches caused him to realise that growth is a natural consequence of health. His latest book, *The Healthy Churches' Handbook*, identifies seven marks of a healthy church and also provides a practical guide for giving your own church a health check. The seven marks of a healthy church are:

1. it is energised by faith
2. it has an outward-looking focus
3. it seeks to find out what God wants
4. it faces the cost of change and growth
5. it operates as a community
6. it makes room for all
7. it does a few things and does them well.[2]

Any church wanting to develop a ministry of evangelism will benefit from seeing how it can be a natural part of what it means to be a healthy church.

The following famous quotation from Lesslie Newbigin makes the same striking point about how we as the church will reveal or obscure the gospel:

> How is it possible that the gospel should be credible, that people should come to believe that the power which has the last word in human affairs is represented by a man hanging on a cross? I am suggesting that the only answer, the only hermeneutic of the gospel, is a congregation of men and women who believe it and live by it.[3]

PURPOSE

There is an important sense in which the vision of God's purposes for the world is something *given*. The Christian faith is a revealed faith. Of course we must interpret what God has given us, and of course we will discover new insights as the Holy Spirit leads us deeper into the truth of this revelation, but the revelation itself, the basic truths that go to make up Christian faith, is not something we decide upon: it is something we have received.

In the Diocese of Oxford, where I now serve, great emphasis is placed on God's purposes for the world in our *Developing Servant Leaders* programme. Christian vision is God's vision for God's world and therefore ought to be recognisably the same for all Christians in all ages and contexts.[4] In a memorable phrase, Bill Hybels, the leader of the Willow Creek church in Chicago, has said, 'Vision is the picture of the future that produces passion.'

In trying to develop servant leadership at the heart of the church we identify a pattern of working which we hope will help our churches grow. This pattern is also relevant as we look at developing a ministry of evangelism in the church. There are three concepts:

- vision
- purpose
- strategy.

Vision is something that is given; purpose is something we work out in response to the vision. Vision is like the mountain top to which we are climbing; purpose is the pathway we choose to take (recognising there may be more than one, and making decisions about the way we won't go just as much as the way we will). Strategy is the short-term plans we make resulting in the action we take: the individual steps that make up the journey.

Another important concept that sits alongside these three concepts is referred to as alignment. Alignment is concerned with bringing into harmony all the various aspects of the organisation (people, structures, finances, decision making – in this case the church) so that the vision, purpose and strategy can be worked through.

In the programme we use the following image to illustrate the whole process: imagine a wall with something that is desired waiting at the top. This is the vision. The ladder that you place against the wall is your purpose: your chosen way of realising the vision. The rungs on the ladder are the individual objectives that are needed in order to ascend the ladder. The precise order of the rungs also gives these objectives priority. Alignment is needed so that the plans you make ensure that there are people available with the time and ability to climb ladders!

You will find similar ideas (and a seemingly infinite variety of jargon!) in all kinds of books on leadership and management. But this terminology seems to be serving the church well, and fits in with a Christian understanding of leadership. It is about how vision is turned into purposeful action. Most of it is applied common sense. Nevertheless, it is astonishing how often we in the church fail to take a strategic approach.

Where the image breaks down is that it seems to present in a linear form what is in reality a more complex and diffuse process. Nevertheless the basic ideas are extremely helpful and underpin the whole of this book. Part One of the book is about vision: about how we receive vision and how we begin to let it shape our life. Part Two is concerned chiefly with purpose: mapping the choices we need to make about the longer-term development of an evangelising church. But in each chapter there are examples of how these ideas have been worked through in the strategies and plans of individual churches.

So if the heart of the vision that God reveals to us as we live our lives in relationship with him is one of *koinonia* – community – then what are the purposes of an evangelising church that seeks to live out this vision in such a way that others are included in the community of God? And what kind of church are we called to be?

3

WHAT KIND OF CHURCH DOES GOD WANT US TO BE?

THE CHURCH IS THE PRIMARY AGENT of God's mission in the world. The church – that is the community of men and women who make up the Christian community – reveals the Christian faith by the life they live. This is a community created by the evangelising ministry of Christ and by the Spirit. It is a community sustained and sent out by that same Spirit. How we are the church will be pivotal to our effectiveness as agents of God's mission. This is not to say that it is our work, but that our willingness to co-operate with God and allow our lives to be shaped by his purposes will go a long way to determining the fruitfulness of our ministry. As Lesslie Newbigin was quoted as saying in the last chapter: 'the only hermeneutic of the gospel is a congregation of men and women who believe it and live by it.'

For catholic Christians this formation in the Christian life will happen most obviously at the Eucharist, the place more than any other where we receive and understand God's purposes for the world. Here we discover what it is to be the church. And as we gather at the Eucharist Sunday by Sunday we declare our faith in a church which is 'holy, catholic and apostolic'.[1] This is the vision for the church that we have received. It is of a church which is united, a church which is holy, a church which is universal and a church with a mission in the world. However, this bright vision often appears lost in the day-to-day business of being the church in practice. Too often all our energy seems to go into the wrong things. We appear obsessed by secondary issues, concerned only with keeping the show on the road and forgetful of why we are here in the first place. It is when this occurs that the church often drives people away from the gospel.

But, despite all its problems, the church remains united not because of its fabulous achievements or holy living, but because it is the body of Christ. Its unity is itself both a given and a gift. It is a given because it is the body of Christ and we are limbs and organs of that body. It is a gift because the community that the church offers to the world is a life lived in unity with God. Hence, it is the one church of Jesus Christ and, despite all its weaknesses and failings, it is the body in whose company and teaching we find communion with God. Even though this beautiful gospel is so often barely visible, it is a saving truth that shapes and sustains the church throughout history as we constantly reset the compass of our discipleship allowing our purposes to be shaped by God's vision.

So, if the vision is for 'one holy, catholic and apostolic church' and if the heart of this vision is the word 'one' itself – an inclusive vision of unity and community – then what do the words 'holy, catholic and apostolic' mean for the purpose and strategy of the church today?

- To be **holy** means to be in *communion with God*. We are holy because of what God has done for us and made possible for us in Christ. It is therefore a church which is centred on God and for whom worship is a priority.
- To be **catholic** means to be in *community with each other.* The word 'catholic' does not just mean universal. The literal meaning is 'that which accords to wholeness'. It is about the quality of our life within the body of Christ. It is therefore a church which is serious about Christian discipleship and for whom the nurture of Christian community and discipleship is a priority.
- To be **apostolic** means to be in *communication with the world.* The word 'apostolic' doesn't only refer to the church being built upon the foundation of the apostles but also reminds us that we are the church that is sent out by God to share his mission. It is therefore a church orientated towards the world and its needs and for whom outreach – service and evangelism – is a priority.

And all the time it is one church, striving to be faithful to the inheritance that has been received and determined to strengthen the unity we have with each other in Christ and the unity God desires for the whole of creation.

This is the church God intends us to *be*. It is our vision. It is what he gives us and establishes for us in Christ. What we *do* as the church – our purpose – arises out of it.

Figure 1: A model for the evangelising (missionary) church

The evangelising church – the church that is participating in God's mission – has three priorities: worship, nurture and outreach. Together these form the mission of the church for they encompass our primary call – to worship God and be in relationship with him – and our primary commission – to make disciples. Making disciples involves outreach and nurture. We are to share with others the fullness of the life we have received.

I have preferred the word 'outreach' to 'evangelism' in the third circle, because the ministry of communicating the gospel includes, but is more than, the ministry of evangelism. Before we can begin to look at this ministry in more practical detail we need to see how it relates to the larger vision. Evangelism is a particular ministry within the whole mission of God's church. It is not something that certain Christians do. It is a ministry which belongs to the whole body. It flows from our defining vision and purpose. Without it, there would be no church at all. All of us are part of the church because we have been evangelised. Although we can all trade stories of inappropriate and unhelpful evangelism, the testimony of our own experience tells us that appropriate and helpful evangelism does go on. We are living proof of it, and the stories of our own journeys to faith should encourage us to understand the ministry we are seeking to develop.

By observing the overlaps, we can also see the evangelising potential of all we do. The different areas of church life are not sealed compartments. They flow into each other. We are made for community with God, hence the life of worship fulfils our life in Christ, but this worship can never be a private affair. It overflows with love and service to the world.[3]

Most of this book is concerned with developing a very specific evangelistic ministry. However, as the book goes on I hope it will be very clear to see how what is most interesting happens in the overlaps. For instance, the model of evangelisation that I am concentrating on in Part Two of the book is one which links together evangelism and nurture, outreach and community. It is through hospitality, welcome and enabling people to belong that we best help them make a journey to faith. The final chapter of the book is a discussion of the relationship between evangelism and worship. Although catholic Christians have always believed in the evangelising power of worship, I believe we have rather lost our nerve and need to look afresh not just at how we worship at the moment, but at the different ways we could be worshipping. This also links in with the challenges of the *Mission-Shaped Church* report to evangelise through developing fresh expressions of Christian community. Many of these will be worship based and will be communities of faith formed in the networks of our society, reaching out through worship.

At the heart of the diagram – and notice that the outline of the overlapping circles creates a heart – is the given vision of the Christian faith: it is what God has done in Jesus Christ that has made communion with God possible, and it is through a life lived in Christ that we can enjoy communion with God, new community with each other, and a new service and communication with the world. This is the 'oneness' of the church. We are also reminded of the scripture with which the book begins, which points us to the truth that it is out of what we know and receive in our hearts that our mouths speak, our priorities are decided and our strategies formed.

Figure 1 can also be used as a tool for analysing church life. It does not take long to list the different activities and programmes of the church within each of the three circles under the headings of 'worship', 'nurture' and 'outreach', helping us discern what we do in terms of our primary vocations. It is interesting that many churches discover that they are doing quite a lot of outreach, but often it is disconnected from their worship and nurture. And often there is very little happening at all in the nurture circle, which is concerned with building community and nurturing discipleship.

MAKING THE FIRST STEP

We have seen that the church that wants to pursue God's vision will embrace its threefold vocation of worship, nurture and outreach. There is one vision, but many possible expressions of it. Each church will choose its own particular pathways through which it chooses to give tangible expression to the vision. It will then need to develop a strategy to identify the actual steps that are needed to make it happen.

What follows is a practical suggestion about how a church might rediscover its missionary calling by producing a simple purpose statement that would be its own particular response to the call to be holy, catholic and apostolic.

Many churches imagine the choice facing them is between 'changing' or 'staying the same'. This is not so. One thing is certain: things will change. The real choice is between shaping the change or being shaped by it. A purpose statement is therefore an aid to creative decision-making and management of change, helping us to decide what we stop doing as much as what we start.

A purpose statement is a tool to facilitate planning. Many churches are bad at planning, often because there is no agreed understanding of either vision or purpose. By agreeing on our purpose there is a yardstick by which everything else can be measured, both the external changes in society to which we have to respond, and the internal changes whereby we try to shape our life around the call to be a holy, catholic and apostolic church.

Producing a purpose statement need not be a difficult or lengthy process. It is important that as many members of the church as possible are involved in the initial process, since it is a commonly owned vision for the church which will best enable it to be effective in its management of change and its planning for the future. At the very least the church council needs to be involved at every stage.

Here is a simple four-point plan for producing a purpose statement. It could be the first step towards becoming a missionary church.

1. Ask everyone to finish the following sentence as a way of expressing what the church is for.

> 'The reason we have a church in N———— is ...'

This could be done at the beginning or end of Sunday worship, at an annual church meeting, or at a specially convened meeting, but is best when as many members of the church as possible can participate. It only takes five minutes. What you are after is a simple statement of purpose. A way of helping people into the exercise is to ask what sort of church they think Jesus wants them to be. Of course this can also be the occasion when the given-ness of the vision for being God's church is preached about. Hence we are not looking to impose our own vision but see how God's vision can shape our purpose.

You now have a collection of statements.

2. Empower a small group of people to take away the statements and analyse their content listing the different things mentioned and calculating what things are mentioned the most.

This process is much simpler than it sounds. On the whole it is not about breaking new ground but reminding ourselves of what we have always known but rarely call to mind. You will be surprised how quickly and easily people list the basic characteristics of worship, nurture, service and outreach that make up church life.

You now have a list of those things which will make up the final statement and an indication of what the church considers most important.

3. The same small group drafts an initial statement – or perhaps each member of the group makes a draft or selects or adapts one of the initial sentences which seems representative of the whole.

You now have a draft, or drafts, of your purpose statement.

4. The church council, or another meeting of the whole church, approves or selects (and probably amends) the statement. There will be some important preliminary questions: Has anything been missed out? Is the language as striking and as memorable as possible? Does everyone feel happy with the process so far and included in it?

You now have your purpose statement.

All this could happen over a few weeks. Straightaway you need to put the statement to work. It provides the criteria for your planning and decision-making. It articulates the vision of the church you feel God calls you to be. It starts to inform you of what you are now called to *do*. It would be also good to review what your church is actually doing in the light of how the statement describes your purpose. It can help prune the activity of the church, showing what you should stop doing.

A SERMON: GETTING EVANGELISM ONTO THE AGENDA

I WONDER WHAT GOES THROUGH your head when you hear the word 'evangelism'? Does it conjure up images of manipulation and intimidation? Are you thinking of those appalling American TV-evangelists? Are you shrinking in your seat thinking you are about to be asked to go and knock on people's doors? Well, many people in the Anglican Church have come to this conclusion: evangelism is what other Christians do in other churches, but it's not for us!

I hope this morning, at the very least, to give you another take on the ministry of evangelism and begin to help us see why we should and could evangelise.

First of all, let's begin with the word itself: it means to share good news, and this is something we human beings do all the time. If you see a good film, or read a good book, if your football team wins, or if a new child is born into your family, you tell others about it. You evangelise them, in the sense that you share your good news. Therefore, if I feel impossibly reticent about ever sharing anything about my Christian faith with anyone, then the first question I need to face is, have I received the Christian faith as good news for my life?

Anyway, I've got some good news to share with you. Effective and appropriate evangelism is happening in the Church of England, in this diocese and even in this parish, and gathered here this morning are about 100 living examples of good and appropriate and effective evangelism having happened! You may never have thought about it like this before, but the reason you are here is that once upon a time you were evangelised. Someone shared the Christian faith with you in such a way that you responded and are now part of Christ's Church. It might have been that you were brought up within the embrace of a loving Christian family, and that's how you came to faith, in which case that was evangelism, that was how you received the faith. It may be that something else happened in your life to bring you into the life of the Church. That was evangelism. It is happening; we just want it to happen more effectively and more appropriately so that more people can come to discover what we have found in Christ.

So let me tell you the story of how one person here this morning got to be a Christian. I'll tell you my story.

I wasn't brought up going to church. I was part of a loving family and I was brought up with Christian values and some sense that there was a God and this mattered. I was 'done' as a baby: I was baptised, but apart from this there was basically no church in my life. My parents were part of that great post-war lapsed generation. They had gone to church as children but when they married and set up home they stopped going. They never rejected the Christian faith; they just got out of the habit.

I owe my Christian faith to the Girl Guide movement! My sister, when she was about eleven, joined the Girl Guides and was required to go to a church parade service once a month. She, and a small group of friends, liked what they found at the church parade and started going along on the other Sundays in-between, got confirmed and joined the church. Now this pricked my parents' conscience (as I said, they never actually rejected the Christian faith) so they started going along to church. My little brother was still little enough to be told what to do, so he got taken to church, leaving me and my big brother back home, in bed, on a Sunday morning flying the flag for agnosticism. With my mother poking her head round the bedroom door asking whether we were coming to church or not. Well, my elder brother was the first to give way and, would you believe it, he started going as well.

This was serious bad news. Here I was in the tender years of adolescence, confused enough with the hormones racing around me, and now my family had got religion big time.

At which point in the story I wish I could remember what it was that made me go for the first time. There was a girl I fancied, who I had discovered went to church, and this was, shall we say, a motivating factor. We also used to have terrific rows about religion over Sunday lunch and maybe I thought, if I go along and discover just how awful it really is, I will have some ammunition to fire at them during our discussions. Anyway, whatever the reason, aged about thirteen, I go to church for what is effectively the first time. And the other thing you need to remember is that I went to church for the first time fairly determined not to like it. And what do I find?

Well, the church I went to – though I didn't realise it at the time, I thought this was what all churches were like – was a church of a fairly high catholic tradition: bells and smells, the full works: proper church. And I didn't understand any of it. But I do remember how it felt. Up until that point, like most people, I had been living my life as if I was the centre of the universe. I loved and valued and appreciated other people, but there was a sense in which other people were only walk-on parts in the central story of the universe which was, of course, my life. But here in this place, not only was I not the centre of attention, no one was. Everything that happened here was focused beyond itself. And how do we describe what I can only call 'the otherness' of God that we experience in worship? This is where words fail us. But it did have an impact.

The other thing I found in this church was powerful preaching. The curate at the time was an ex-Durham miner and a great big Old Testament prophet of a priest. Again, I don't really remember what he said, and I don't know whether you have ever had this experience, but when he spoke it seemed like he was speaking directly to me, challenging me about what I was going to do with my life: this one life that God had given me. And somehow the combination of the otherness of God in the worship and the absolute here-and-now-ness of God in the preaching ensnared me, and I found myself saying with Peter (though I didn't know these words at the time), 'Lord, to whom can we go? You have the words of eternal life' (John 6:68).

Well, that wasn't the end of my story, just the beginning, but as I look back over my story there are several conclusions I draw. First of all, what attracted me to the Christian faith and what keeps me in the Christian faith is God. It was the reality and beauty of God that drew me and that sustains me. But it was God working his purposes out through his church. It seems that God has woven into the story of how I became a Christian the witness of many other Christian people. First, there was my sister, aged eleven: I don't remember my sister ever saying anything to me about her new-found faith, and yet her silent witness brought faith to all our family. Then there were those Girl Guide leaders, whom I barely knew. They must have been pretty incredible people that they had so communicated the reality of faith to that small group of girls that the repercussions of their ministry are still felt in my life today. Then there was that church; even though I don't remember much about it, it must have been a welcoming church, and the worship and preaching in that church had relevance, integrity and vigour. Put all that together: the witness of ordinary Christian people in their daily lives, the service and action of the church in the community, worship that inspires, and preaching that relates faith to life. And evangelism happens, Christ is made known.

One more thing: you know in your family you have people that you call 'auntie' and 'uncle', but they're not really your auntie and uncle. Well, in my family we had my Auntie Millie: she wasn't my auntie; she was my grandma's best friend. My Auntie Millie was a devout Roman Catholic, the sort of devout Roman Catholic who went to Mass pretty much every day of her life. When I was ordained as a Deacon she came to the ordination, which for her, as a certain sort of Roman Catholic, was quite a big step to take: she had never before been to worship in a non-Roman Catholic Church. But she came to the service and she was pleased for me, and after the service she came to the party, and she bought me a present – a book of Cardinal Hume's sermons – and this is what she told me: every day, for the past forty years, when she had gone to Mass, she had prayed for the conversion of my family. And on this day even my Auntie Millie was probably prepared to concede that being in the Church of England was an acceptable second best.

Now I don't understand the mystery of how God uses our prayers to make his purposes known, but I believe that one of the reasons I am here, speaking to you today, is because of my Auntie Millie's prayers.

Evangelism is God's work. But it is God's work in which we each have a part to play – as individuals and as Christian communities. And just as God has written into my life the witness of many others, so now he wants to write our witness into other people's lives. According to our different personalities, gifts and circumstances each of us has a part to play in God's work of evangelism.

A CONVERSATION IN THE PUB
AFTER THE SERVICE

After the service Fr Stephen, Mike, the churchwarden, Roz, the youth worker, Beth, in her late twenties and a new member of the congregation, and Yvonne, secretary to the PCC and a longstanding pillar of the church, go for a drink.

Having bought their drinks they sit down together for a chat.

BETH: I've never really thought of evangelism like that before. I mean, I always thought it was knocking on doors, big rallies, you know, badgering people with God.

MIKE: Yes. Billy Graham and all that.

ROZ: I'm surprised to hear you say that, Beth, after all you've only been coming to the church a short while yourself and that wasn't how you came to faith.

BETH: No, I suppose not. It's just that I never really thought of what happened to me as evangelism. I mean evangelism . . . it sounds so awful. You wouldn't do it to your worst enemy.

ROZ: Yes, but what happened to you was good, wasn't it?

BETH: It was. I mean, I don't know what I would have done if the church hadn't been there to help me. I thought my little girl was going to die. Meningitis is really frightening, and when they said, did I want to see the hospital chaplain, well, actually I didn't, most of me wanted to run a mile. After all I was thinking: if there is a God he wouldn't let this stuff happen in the first place. But then there was a little bit of me – just a little bit – which wanted to believe and wanted to hope, and I was really desperate, and so I said yes.

He didn't really help that much. In fact he didn't really say anything. But his presence, and just the fact that he came at all and gave us some time, well that helped. And then she got better and I didn't really give it any thought, until that time the church was running a holiday club. Usually I wouldn't have anything to do with that sort of thing, but I suppose I just kind of felt well disposed towards the church, able to give it a chance. So when Emily came home from school saying she'd been invited, I thought why not? Well, you know the rest.

ROZ: Yes, I remember you coming to pick Emily up each day and being really suspicious of what was going on and never coming in. But then on the last day you came early and saw what they were doing and I said, why not come along on Sunday... and of course you didn't!

BETH: No, not that Sunday.

ROZ: But a few weeks later ...

BETH: Yes, I came ...

ROZ: Why was it? You've never told me.

BETH: It's strange really. It was something on the local news on Saturday evening. You know, that bit after the main news where they tell you all the local stuff, usually really boring, like someone's left their brolly on the bus, or a cat's got stuck up a tree. Well, there was something about a child being molested. It was really horrific, and I just thought, like a real stab to my heart – this world is so screwed up – excuse me, Father – and all of a sudden I thought I must do something; do something so that I can be a better person. You know, put something back.

FR STEPHEN: So that was what made you come along?

BETH: Yes, that and so much other stuff. And then I didn't understand it all.

MIKE: And joined our wonderful nurture group.

BETH: Yes, Mike, I really found that helpful, though it took a while to pluck up the courage to join.

MIKE: Yes, I must have asked you a thousand times.

YVONNE: (*Sarcastically*) I'm sure that really helped!

BETH: Well, eventually I said yes and slowly it started to make sense.

ROZ: And we call that evangelism.

BETH: I don't. I call it discovering.

ROZ: Which is fine, we don't have to call it anything. But what you experienced, all that stuff which led you to church and led you to God, that's evangelism, and what we need to do in this church is not so much different things, but make the connections between all the things we already do. Like Mike runs his group, and loads of people have been helped in their faith through that and have joined the church, but we don't always make the most of the opportunities we have through holiday clubs and other stuff we do in the community to encourage people to sign up.

YVONNE: Yes, and Mike hassles people so much about it they'd probably prefer to join the Jehovah's Witnesses.

MIKE: Why are we all getting at me? I'm keen.

YVONNE: Yes, too keen. It frightens people away.

FR STEPHEN: Keen is good, Mike, but we have to start where people are. And for most people that's a long way off.

ROZ: But we have so many good things going for us and so many opportunities. If we could just co-ordinate a bit more, and maybe do one or two things that would gather people together. I think there are lots of people in this parish like Beth, who want to find out more, who are asking questions of life, but don't know what to do, and we don't know how to connect with them.

YVONNE: Not to mention the people we lose!

FR STEPHEN: That is a problem.

MIKE: I still hate it that my kids have stopped coming.

ROZ: But that's also part of the problem. We still keep thinking the journey must lead to church on Sunday morning. The journey is to God, and we need to find ways of being the church that will help people make the journey. I mean why would a young person, interested in finding God, but knowing nothing about the church, come to us on Sunday morning? We need to be a different sort of church.

YVONNE: What! Change our way of doing things?

ROZ: Not necessarily. But do different things as well. What feeds and nurtures our faith won't necessarily work for everyone.

YVONNE: I'm not always sure it works for me. I love it, but if I'm honest I love the security it brings me, the nostalgia... I don't know what actual faith I've got. It's the church I love, not the gospel.

There is a silence.

YVONNE: Oh, I know you're all thinking what a terrible person, but there, I've said it now, and I don't think I'm the only one who thinks it. Church means a lot to us. It's what we know. It's our security, and it's not that we don't want anyone else coming, it's just that we can't bear to see it change, not now, not after so long...

FR STEPHEN: But you don't want to see it die?

YVONNE: No. And I don't want to see it bankrupt either, so at the very least it would be good to get a few new people in to help pay the bills!

ROZ: But you know it doesn't work like that.

YVONNE: Yes, of course I do. But all this talk of evangelism and Mike going on about his blessed nurture group, it gives me the creeps. Why don't people just come to church? What's wrong with them?

FR STEPHEN: Well, they do come. Beth has come, and she has brought some of her friends. It just doesn't always happen in the ways we imagine, and we have to find the ways of helping people. It's our job!

YVONNE: I know. I know. Just don't ask me to like it!

FR STEPHEN: No one is. But we do need to see that what is asked of us is not my idea, or Roz's idea, but what God is calling us to do. This is his church, not ours.

MIKE: It is something we need to pray about.

YVONNE: Jesus, Joseph and Mary! Don't go all evangelical on me. We are not praying in the pub! That's where I draw the line.

MIKE: I didn't mean here – though I can't see what's wrong with it – I mean, we need to pray that God will make faith real for us. Then we will find the ways of sharing it with others that work. We can't give what we haven't got.

I know I come over all confident and sure of my faith, but if I'm honest sometimes that's because I'm so full of doubts and anxieties that I feel I need to convert myself, and if I could just do this, then I could convert others. But I know that's all the wrong way round, and it makes me seem insensitive. Only God converts, and really if I quietened down a bit and listened a bit more and let God do his stuff, then the church would be in a much healthier state. We need to be a receiving church before we can be a sharing church.

YVONNE: I'll drink to that! And I'll tell you what, Mike: I'll even pray about it. Though not here. That's not my way; but when I come to Mass each day, even if my reasons for coming are all muddled, I'll pray for this church and for its mission. Just like your Auntie Millie, Father. Now don't ask for more!

FR STEPHEN: We couldn't.

They all pause, and take long gulps of their drink.

MIKE: There's so much we need to learn: about the world we live in, about the questions people are asking, about the faith itself ...

ROZ: And about the sort of church God wants us to be.

BETH: I think this is a really good church. It keeps asking questions. It listened to mine.

INTERMISSION: THE CULTURE
IN WHICH WE EVANGELISE AND
THE WAYS WE RESPOND

WE NEED TO TAKE CAREFUL ACCOUNT OF the world in which we are set. God's purposes are unchanging. Hence the mission of the church – or rather our participation in God's mission – is an agenda for the world which does not change. In every age God wishes to bring wholeness, peace and harmony to the creation he has made. He does this by shaping our will and by drawing us into relationship with him. However, in each generation the challenges of this mission need to be discovered afresh, and in facing the new questions that a new culture poses, new insights and depths of faith are discovered.

Until recently I served at Peterborough Cathedral. While I was there a terrible fire nearly destroyed the building. A massive programme of cleaning and restoration followed in which several mediaeval wall paintings were discovered. As a consequence the guidebooks introducing visitors to the Cathedral will have to be re-written and the cathedral guides re-trained. It is not that a new truth is being added, but something that was always there, and always part of the historic reality, has only now, in this generation, been revealed afresh. Such a process of rediscovery and re-expression is constantly going on in the life of the church. Too often, we settle for preaching the gospel *again* in each generation, when our vocation is to proclaim it *afresh*.[1] The missionary church which takes its agenda from God's purposes in the world will always be asking purpose questions: What kind of church does God want us to be? How can we give this proper expression in our own culture and with the circumstances and resources of our own life together and with the particular people that God has called to be part of this congregation? How does our being the church communicate and reveal the purposes of God? And what do the questions and issues that our society poses reveal to us about the very nature of the gospel itself? The asking of such questions is not about creating a more palatable gospel in order to be successful in the world, but about allowing the concerns of the world to be the refining fire through which the Spirit continues to lead us into all truth.

About this process, Archbishop Rowan Williams comments:

> believing in the Church Catholic must mean believing in the Church Penitent ... our continuity with the Christian past lies not in repeating what earlier generations said but bringing ourselves before the same point of judgement and asking, with them, for conversion – which may mean that we do and say things they did not.[2]

Taking the example, of slavery he adds:

> The Church before and after its general change of heart on slavery is not two different churches; the post-emancipation church had received from the pre-emancipation church a faith which had depth and resources enough to put its own history in question because it had received the knowledge of a God faithful, merciful and inexorably demanding truthfulness ... Change is only betrayal if we forget that the centre of tradition, the heart of what we hand on as saving faith, is the possibility of new beginnings and the truth that our errors of interpretation are not the last word in a community which exists because of a belief in the indestructibility of God's commitment.[3]

This is the church God wants us to be: a church tenaciously committed to the truth. It is the truth that will set us free. It is the truth that the Spirit is constantly leading us to discover and rediscover. If the sad experiences of the past couple of years, where various fissures of disagreement have opened up over our response to the questions gay and lesbian people pose the church, lead us to a more careful reading of Scripture and a more careful examination of our tradition, then there is good reason to be hopeful that, beyond our present impasse, the Spirit is preparing us to be a more inclusive church, even if, at the moment, we find it hard to imagine what this will look like.

The *Windsor Report* itself made a similar point:

> The current crisis thus constitutes a call to the whole Anglican Communion to re-evaluate the ways in which we have read, heard, studied and digested scripture. We can no longer be content to drop random texts into arguments, imagining that the point is thereby proved, or indeed to sweep away sections of the New Testament as irrelevant to today's world, imagining that problems are thereby solved. We need mature study, wise and prayerful discussion, and a joint commitment to hearing and obeying God as he speaks to us in scripture, to discovering more of the Jesus to whom all authority is committed, and to being open to the fresh wind of the Spirit who

inspired scripture to be written in the first place. If our present difficulties force us to read and learn together from scripture in new ways, they will not have been without profit.[4]

Another danger, however, is that we get so hung up on questions concerning human sexuality that we appear absurd to the world around us or indifferent to all the other questions the world faces. This world is changing rapidly. For centuries we lived in a comparatively stable society where the model for being the church was based around an understanding of our culture and society as being basically Christian. Our job, as the church, was to teach people the faith and care for them. We understood our role in a predominantly pastoral way. But there is very little sense in now calling Britain a Christian country. This is not just a matter of Sunday trading laws – though it is remarkable how the nature of Sunday has been transformed in a matter of years – it is about the whole way we feel about ourselves, and the very different ways we choose to gain identity and purpose for life. Even forty years ago, when I had just about started at school, though I was not part of a churchgoing family, I was brought up with some awareness that I was part of a Christian country and shared in a commonly owned set of beliefs and values. This is not the same today. The very fact that we describe our society as *post*-modern says more about what we are leaving behind than what we are entering into.

We live in a questioning society that is highly suspicious of the big, all-embracing answers of the past. For many people Christianity takes its place on the back burner of history, along with many of the other ideologies that played such a large part in shaping the life and aspirations of the last couple of centuries.

Into this vacuum has come a whole variety of other ways of making sense of life. Be it a high-fibre diet and plenty of exercise, Zen Buddhism or psycho-analysis, there is a great deal of evidence to show that people still thirst for meaning in their lives. What has changed is that there is no one all-embracing spiritual, psychological, or for that matter political or economic philosophy, which a majority of people look to. The society in which we live is both pluralist and relativist. I do not mean this in any pejorative sense. This is just a description of the way we are: there are many truths to look to, and what is true for me may not be true for you. As Louis MacNeice observed, 'the world is crazier and more of it than we think. Incorrigibly plural'.[5] It is unlikely that this poem could have been written before the Somme, Auschwitz and finally Hiroshima blew away the optimistic certainties of the Enlightenment. In our own day the meticulously conceived and very humanly executed horror of September 11th and the mighty, uncontrollable and unpredictable rush of the Asian Tsunami make the world seem even more fragile and randomly hateful. There is no big meaning or comfort to be found, only the little self-contained and individual meanings I can salvage for myself and cocoon myself away with.

This is the world the church finds itself in. A common image for it is the supermarket (after all, shopping seems to be the great pastime of the post-modern world). There are many ways to find meaning in life and they are all laid out on the supermarket shelves; but, and here is the rub, no one thing has any greater claim to truth than another. All are welcome to display their wares so long as they do not oppress the rival claims of others by declaring a universal truth. In fact, it is this claiming of universality which is the very thing our age is recoiling from. 'Post-modern' and 'post-enlightenment' are better described as 'post-ideological'. Christianity is seen as one ideology among many. It is fine for you to believe those things provided you do not claim that the ideas that help you find purpose in your life have an equal claim on mine.

Perhaps an even better image would be the Internet – this vast sprawling spider's web of information appears to be a force of liberation, giving us access to everything and everyone, but lacks the authority and discernment to give us the guidance we require to find what we need. In appearing to have everything we find we have virtually nothing. And, anyway, half the traffic on the information highway is pornographic. Aching with thirst for a few drops of wisdom, we drown in a tide of information, only two clicks away from what is most appalling in our nature, and as far away as ever from the guidance and affirmation we crave.

Even this very brief look at the kind of culture in which we are called to evangelise shows with harsh clarity the main problems facing the Church. We believe the gospel of Jesus Christ is the saving truth for all people of all ages, yet we are living in an age which is increasingly suspicious of anybody who makes universal claims for anything. Here I am not just talking about religious claims: there is a growing relativism towards all commonly held beliefs about the world, and this affects science, religion, literature and all schools of human thought. The reaction against the optimism of the Enlightenment is an attack on rationalism of any kind. This is truly the 'new age' we hear so much about. Meanwhile, all kinds of other forces in our society numb our senses, compromise our morality and appeal to what is most base and vulgar within us.

Little wonder that at the end of the second Christian millennium all the major Christian Churches called for a decade of evangelism! However, even from the perspective of a few years this well-intentioned initiative looks a bit like the Church operating in all-too-familiar 'First World War general mode': one more push, boys, and we'll be in Berlin by Christmas!

And yet we are being mown down. The forces at work in our culture to make us understand ourselves as isolated individuals have not stopped us longing for meaning and purpose in our lives. We need this just as much as any human being in history. But it presents a smorgasbord of reality in which just trying to shout louder than all the rest will not make us more attractive. Whether we like it or not, we must take our place alongside other ways of making sense of life. It is this shift in the culture which makes the ministry of evangelism seem so hard and sometimes pointless.

But the decade of evangelism did teach us something. First, it helped us think more creatively about the content of the gospel we share. Second, it helped us to rediscover the basic truth that for most people becoming a Christian is like a journey. It reminded us that for most people belonging comes before believing, and how being an attractive, healthy and welcoming church is a vital part of any strategy for evangelism. Third, it forced us to look at the very shape the church takes to see how the cultures in which we live require flexibility and a creativity that will enable the life of the gospel, and the Christian communities which live it, to find fresh expression.

Billy Connolly once said, 'There's no such thing as bad weather, only the wrong clothes.' These are prophetic words for the church, as we seek to discover what will be the cultural clothes in which the message of the gospel needs to be dressed for the culture in which we evangelise today. Hence the strategy that follows in the rest of this book is built around a model for evangelism that is motivated by God's vision for the world, nourished by prayer, rooted in service, and accepting that there will be many ways forward and no one-size-fits-all solutions. And we will measure our success not by our fruitfulness but our faithfulness. Though we do long to be fruitful: the world needs what the gospel brings.

But even without the changing culture which gives a wide berth to the universal claims of Christian faith, and the challenge to find new ways of being the church, busy clergy and committed Christian people are being asked to change the way they think about the church's ministry. No longer is church just about caring for people and teaching them the faith – the pastoral model I alluded to above. We have now got to find people in the first place! But the reason we do this is not just because we need to survive, and even less because we are ambitious for success; we do it out of faithfulness to the Lord's command to make disciples, and because we always hold on to the interrelationship between the ministry of evangelism and God's work of mission into which the church is called. It is for the sake of the kingdom – God's vision for a renewed humanity and a renewed creation – that we evangelise. We are welcoming people into relationship with God as citizens of God's kingdom; not recruiting members to a cash-strapped organisation. Getting this motivation the right way round is hugely important. The work of evangelism is the work of God.

A RESPONSIVE CHURCH

There is no need to despair. It is the first time for a long time that we have been in a situation like this, but it is *not* the first time. The pluralism of our multi-faith society has some interesting similarities with the world of the Roman Empire into which the Christian faith was born. Then the Christian faith had to jostle and harry alongside many other philosophies and religions. In the end it won the day for three distinctive reasons:

1. the credibility and intellectual integrity of the faith that was being shared;
2. the ability of faith to clothe itself in the various cultures it encountered;
3. the evidence in people's lives for the veracity and transforming energy of the gospel.

In other words, the work of evangelism (the making known of the gospel of Jesus Christ) was woven tightly together with apologetics (the reasoning, arguing and commending of faith) and spirituality (the lived experience of Christian life).

These are issues we will return to, but the point I want to make here is that evangelism was effective because it was bound up with being a church in mission. It was conscious of its great commission, but untarnished by either the triumphalism that would seek to ride roughshod over other strongly held beliefs, or the complacency which merely waits for people to come to you. In those first centuries the church had either to be a missionary church or not a church at all.

PASTORAL EVANGELISM

It is not that in today's situation the pastoral ministry of caring for people and teaching them the faith is unimportant, but that it is necessary to locate this ministry within the missionary dynamic. As we rediscover how to do evangelism, we must also relearn apologetics and re-energise our spirituality. This will mean more pastoral care, not less. In this respect some of the slogans which have been used about evangelism in the past have served us poorly. We have been told that we should move from maintenance to mission and from pastoral care to evangelism. But these are false distinctions. We cannot simply stop maintaining the church as we have inherited it from the past; neither can, nor should, we stop caring for each other. Not only is the quality of our caring relationships one of the biggest attractions to the Christian life, but any priest will tell you that the first fruit of evangelism is more pastoral care! We need to maintain the church as we have inherited it, and at the same time plant and nurture the church of the future. With regard to pastoral care I want to argue that

our problem is that we have not been pastoral enough! We have either seen
pastoral care as entirely separate from evangelism or, even where there is
a connection, allowed pastoral care to become something much less than
the nurture of a Christian community which is its main purpose. It has
become highly individualised: one individual – usually the priest –
looking after all the other individuals. It has not been *one another care*
within the body of the church, neither has it been about body building:
growing a Christian community in faith and love, the real business of
being a caring church.

Being a priest today is a tough job. But our models for ministry need to
reflect the reality of God who is Father, Son and Holy Spirit.[6] We need a
much more collaborative pattern of ministry, with the priest as the
animator of the Body so that the pastoral and evangelistic ministries
become part of the one ministry of the one church. The missionary church
is also the pastoral church.

SAVING TRUTH

The Church of the first few centuries displayed an astonishing commitment to the truth of the gospel. Many people died rather than deny that
truth. It would have seemed like fanaticism were it not for the gracious
humility with which people turned the other cheek and offered forgiveness
to those who persecuted them. We need that kind of commitment. Unless
we are a church which is committed to the truth, then, to put it crudely,
there will be no one to teach and no one to care for and no church at all.
We must believe that our faith, without standing in unnecessary judgement
on other beliefs and ideas, holds life-and-death truth for every human
being. We must be prepared to live by this truth and share it with others.
It is wise to remember that the church is always only one generation away
from extinction.

What is needed is a change of mindset. We no longer live in
Christendom. We are not the only item on the supermarket shelf. It is not
self-evidently the case that we are the best item on offer. Certainly, we are
not the most attractive. Our faith makes huge claims about itself and
massive demands on those who follow in its way. Therefore this is one
book about evangelism which will not argue that what is required is
simply a jazzy repackaging to solve all our ills or, worse, a redesign of the
product itself. A theme running through this book is the *spirituality* of
evangelism. We follow a crucified Lord: Jesus by all present-day standards
of church growth and evangelism was something of a failure. By arguing
that we become a missionary church I am not exhorting us to become a
'successful' church. That way of thinking is part of our misunderstanding
of evangelism, even if it is often fed by the hard-sell evangelism of

well-intentioned, but over-zealous Christians. We need humility in our evangelism. We are stewards of the gospel for this generation. We need to teach the faith; we need to care for one another within the body of the church; and we also need to share the faith. This is the simple truth of what it means to be a *holy, catholic and apostolic church.*

As we begin to reach out in service to our local communities so the refining fire of people's questions will challenge the credibility of our faith and enable us to speak to the questions our society asks. It is in this way that the Spirit will bring order out of chaos and lead us into truth. The given vision of the gospel remains the same; but there is much about it we still have to learn. The questions that today's culture poses are a vital ingredient in our learning. We serve its needs and we listen carefully to its questions. In this way we will be challenged to find the way of being the church which fits our context, and slowly, in the lives of those who follow Christ, the transforming energy of the gospel will be revealed. What follows is a way of getting started.

PART TWO

THE MINISTRY OF EVANGELISM

4

A MODEL FOR EVANGELISM

WE NEED A MODEL FOR understanding the ministry of evangelism that connects with the culture in which we are evangelising and makes sense of our experience of helping people discover the Christian faith.

For many years the controlling biblical paradigm for evangelism was the story of Paul's encounter on the road to Damascus.[1] Although this beautiful and subtle story clearly places Paul's very dramatic encounter with the Risen Christ in the context of a much longer journey, we tend to think of it only in terms of the extraordinary and the spectacular. In other words it feels a long way away from our usual experience of either sharing the faith or receiving it ourselves. It encouraged the church to think about conversion in terms of a moment of response, and evangelism as somehow catching, or even creating, that moment.

Of course, this also meant that many churches didn't really engage in evangelism at all: we just couldn't imagine being involved in this type of ministry. If we did think about evangelism we saw it like this:

CONTACT

COMMITMENT
CHURCH MEMBERSHIP

Figure 2

According to this view, evangelism is a fairly straightforward process. There are a lot of people 'out there' in the world who are not Christians;

the task of evangelism is to make contact with them and bring them to commitment to Christ and membership of the church.

At first sight this view of evangelism also fits a neat caricature of how some catholic Christians like to view some evangelical Christians. However, the situation is actually more nuanced. Unwittingly many churches of a catholic tradition are also operating this model of evangelism, either through parish missions that place great hope on people coming to faith or returning to faith during a single period of intense evangelistic activity, or simply through the invitation to come and participate in the worship of the church. From the perspective of someone outside the church the invitation to 'be saved' or the invitation 'to come to Mass' appears equally nonsensical. Indeed, the actual experience of those who are coming to faith, makes it hard to believe that evangelism could ever adequately be depicted by a straight line. If we were to depict evangelism diagrammatically we would probably want to draw a long and meandering line. There would be many false starts, cul-de-sacs, wrong turnings and back-tracking. We know that helping people come to faith is rarely an easy or straightforward business. Often it begins with people's pain. There are always obstacles to encounter. But the changed nature of the culture in which we evangelise also means that when we make contact with people today we cannot assume they have any knowledge of the Christian faith and the traditions of the Church. All our jargon is without meaning to them. And they will probably be deeply suspicious of any universal claims to truth that we might make, and ill at ease with the concepts of sin, forgiveness and salvation with which we might try to describe the Christian story and claim its relevance to their life.

In the early 1990s John Finney did some research on how adults become Christians.[2] Several hundred people were interviewed across the spectrum of church tradition and denomination. The overwhelming evidence pointed towards about three-quarters of these people coming to faith gradually over a period of years. This research has been hugely influential in the way Christians of all traditions think about the ministry of evangelism.

The biblical story that best describes this experience of evangelism is the road to Emmaus[3] rather than the road to Damascus. This story also contains a dramatic encounter and a real turning around, but it is more obviously a story of gradual transformation within the context of an accompanied journey. It speaks directly to the situation we find ourselves in today.

None of this comes as great surprise to catholic Christians: we readily talk about the journey of faith. However, we need to recognise that we have tended to talk a good game, rather than actually get involved in the ministry itself. And in order to develop this ministry we need a new model. While it remains true that some people will have the sudden conversion that a straight line depicts, most people will have a long and more complicated path to travel. Between contact and commitment a journey takes place.

So this is what evangelism actually looks like:

CONTACT

NURTURE

COMMITMENT
CHURCH MEMBERSHIP

Figure 3

The word I am using to describe what happens on this journey is 'nurture'. This, of course, is the same word we use to describe how we bring up our children. It is also the same word I used in Part One to describe that part of the church's life which is concerned with community. This is no coincidence. The ministry of nurture involves a lot more than simply proclaiming truths, exhorting people to change, or even teaching them how to live. It is first of all about a safe and affirming environment where you know yourself to be valued and loved, where your questions are taken seriously, where you can grow at your own pace and towards your own potential. It is about helping people to become part of a community and to understand themselves within that community. Churches need to build a place of nurture.

Also by contact I don't just mean contact with the church, but contact with God – or should we say 'the possibility of God'. Although people are still suspicious of the church, they are encountering God in a myriad of different ways: through the birth of a child, or the death of a loved one, the breaking up of a relationship, a change of job, the mountain-top experiences of a beautiful sunset, a star-filled sky or the mist of a newly dawned day.

People are looking for value, meaning and purpose in their lives. They are waking up asking questions about where life is going and what it is about. Many people don't feel as if they have any sense of belonging in a confused and frantic society. People long for community but don't know their next-door neighbour's name. They are having dreams of another way of living. They are having nightmares about where the world is going.

Then there are the books like *The Da Vinci Code* that fly off the shelves and feed an appetite for wonder that is so often starved. And there is the witness of the church in the world: the example of a Christian friend; local projects to alleviate the suffering of the homeless or befriend the elderly; the action to limit the poverty of the world and redress the growing imbalance between rich and poor; the shout of outrage at the way we exploit and abuse our planet.

All this brings people into contact with the possibility of God; it creates a chink in the armour of the secular world view which thought God was no more, but can't help wondering. People, who start out by simply asking questions of life, seeking after a deeper truth and a greater sense of value and purpose, can become fellow travellers with the church, involved in a process of nurture where they can ask their questions and experience something of the true nature of Christian life and the value of the Christian faith. This is real evangelism. The straight line is still there – people who come to faith suddenly – but the emphasis is on the accompanied journey of the curved line. But even when people do come to faith suddenly, as indeed they do (if John Finney's research shows that three-quarters of people come to faith gradually, that still leaves an awful lot of people coming to faith suddenly and dramatically), they still need to be nurtured into their new-found faith.

The phrase 'accompanied journey' comes from the language of the catechumenate. This was the model for evangelism and nurture used by the early Church, where initiation was properly understood as a long-term process. Nor was it just about church membership: the aim was active discipleship. Therefore our diagram needs a further dynamic:

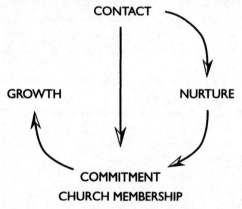

Figure 4

The evangelistic process does not stop when people become members of the local church. It overflows into what I am calling *growth*. This is a massive issue for the Church today. Many members of our congregations are faithful Christians, in so far as they attend church regularly, but they have not grown into that maturity of faith whereby they feel able to live the Christian life Monday to Saturday. Christian faith has never become much more than an important, but nevertheless secondary, adjunct to a basically unchanged life. Church has just become something you attend, when it should be something you are. Growth is stunted.

Evangelism must, therefore, never be satisfied with anything less than the making of disciples, which is Christ's commission. This goes way beyond the standard six-to-ten-week confirmation course which is still the basic model of initiation used in so many churches. We must aim for a changed life. And as we have already noted, becoming a disciple will be much more about growing in relationship with God, through a life of prayer and service, than about growing in our knowledge of God, though this is also important: we need a faith that is intellectually credible.

The effect of a changed life is the living of the Christian life in and for the world. Our diagram can be completed in this way:

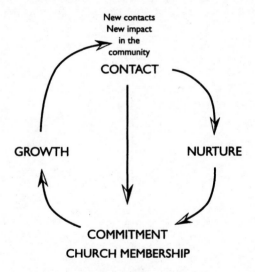

Figure 5: The growth spiral

I call this diagram 'the growth spiral'. It is not a circle going endlessly round and round, but a spiral by which the church grows. As people grow in their own faith so the contact they make with others in the world has a new and provocative impact. The most effective evangelism of all is the Christlike witness of ordinary Christians in their everyday lives.

It is when we try to short-circuit the circle and go only for straight-line evangelism that it becomes the counter-productive and often artificial task that gives the gospel a bad name. When discipleship is seen as the goal of evangelism, witness, service and proclamation flow together in a life properly focused on Christ and on the building of his kingdom. We reach a point where evangelism just happens. It happens not because it has been artificially tacked on to an already busy church programme, but because it is the most natural consequence of a Christian life. We cannot help but put into action the saving truth which now shapes our life. We cannot help but speak of the things we have seen and heard.[4]

PEOPLE ON THE MOVE

I first developed this diagram in the work I did in the 1990s as Missioner in the Wakefield diocese. I have shown it to literally hundreds of churches as an aid to making sense of the ministry of evangelism.[5] Let me offer one further refinement to the diagram where we can see how people move from seeking after meaning in life to sharing in the apostolic vocation of the church. This way of thinking about evangelism is, of course, closely linked to the ministry of spiritual direction in which people are also accompanied on a journey of discovering and deepening faith.

Figure 6

The right-hand side of the diagram is the journey *to* faith. Here people move from being seekers – those who are asking questions of life – to fellow travellers with the church – those who are being nurtured in the way of faith. The left-hand side of the diagram is the journey *of* faith. Here people become Christians and begin the pilgrimage of faith, growing to become those who understand that they have a share in God's mission. I refer to such people as 'apostles', meaning they have a share in the apostolic vocation of the church. Between the two is commitment, where through personal response to God and the initiation rites of the church people enter into the Body of Christ.

Under the old way of thinking about evangelism (but not doing very much about it) all the emphasis was on the straight line down the middle. And we thought it was all up to us: we had to make contact with people, we had to convert them. Now we see that if we accompany people on a process of nurture it will, in God's good time, lead to commitment and church membership, but it is not something we can engineer or control. God is the evangelist.

Secondly, if we enable people to grow in their faith, we see this having a creative impact in the world. In other words, contact and commitment take care of themselves if we get nurture and growth right!

In the following chapters we will travel round this diagram, showing how people can be accompanied from a position of interested unbelief to committed and active discipleship. The actual story of how people come to faith is much more haphazard, but the diagram seems to work because it presents a model of evangelism that flows out of the pastoral ministry churches are already involved in and helps set priorities for developing this ministry. Priorities will differ according to the circumstances of each community. For some churches the urgent task will be to develop a place of nurture. For others it might be renewing the life of the existing congregation. For others it will be developing that first ministry of contact. But at the heart of this way of doing evangelism is the concept of nurture: both building a nurturing place where people can explore faith and developing a nurturing attitude in the way we serve others. We shall look next at building a place of nurture.

Example

St Mary's, Hightown, a church with a strong catholic and liturgical tradition, was a church in decline. Not so much that anyone had really noticed; just a steady getting smaller and older. But when a new priest decided to gather together the statistics over a ten-year period, and when the PCC saw the extent of the decline, and when it was pointed out that there had not been a confirmation in the parish for a couple of years, it was agreed that something should be done. But what? And so things carried on as they were for another year in the vague hope that by being friendly and welcoming new people might come along.

But the following year there were two deaths in the congregation, and these people had been big financial supporters of the church. Not only was the congregation suddenly looking noticeably smaller, now it was getting harder to pay the parish share. This did spur some people into life. The initial reaction was to fund-raise, and though their efforts met with some limited success, it used up huge amounts of time and energy. And with a smallish congregation – about forty adults on an average Sunday and half a dozen children – time and energy were what they didn't really have. The few young adults who worshipped at St Mary's were already extremely pressured.

Also after that there was a sense that the community outside were getting the message that all the church was interested in was their money. While it seemed reasonable to ask the community to support the fabric and upkeep of the church building, there was something uncomfortable about raising money for day-to-day ministry costs. Eventually at a difficult and heated annual meeting, a young woman who was new to the congregation, having moved into the area from another part of the country, asked, 'Why are we here? What is the purpose of this church?'

And this question stopped everyone dead in their tracks. Many of them had been coming to church for so long that they had forgotten why they came. They did want the church to survive and flourish, but when pressed, they didn't really know why. Or they did know, but they had sort of forgotten about it. This led to the Diocesan Stewardship Adviser being invited to come and talk to the parish. She was helpful on matters of planned giving and use of time and talents, but the most helpful thing she did was encourage the church to think about its purpose. And so began a long journey towards growth. The church produced a purpose statement.[6] In fact, once they got started they were surprised how easy it was and how much agreement there was about the purpose of the church. After various deliberations the statement read:

> **St Mary's exists to give Jesus Christ a face in Hightown through the quality of its worship, its fellowship and its mission.**
>
> **St Mary's looks to encourage its members, and the people of the community of which it is a part, to realise their full potential as children of God.**

They then started to use the statement to plan ahead, and it was fairly easy to identify three clear priorities: worship, nurture and outreach. They were also able to relate these to their credal understanding of the church. Worship was about being a holy church. Nurture was about being a catholic church. Outreach was about being an apostolic church.

When they analysed their life in the light of the statement they quickly became aware that very little happened in their church to give Jesus a face through their fellowship with one another. Apart from some occasional social events, Lent groups and the Mother's Union, there was not much else happening. As for evangelism, there was nothing other than the Occasional Offices and a good relationship with the local school. Of their three primary areas of purpose – worship, fellowship and outreach – only worship really took a priority in what actually went on, and even this could hardly be said to give Jesus Christ a face. If they were really honest much of their worship was tired and lifeless.

The striking phrase 'to give Jesus Christ a face', which had come out of one of the first sentences put down by a member of the church, seemed to stand in judgement on much of their church life: could the face of Jesus be seen in their church? The second part of their statement was equally challenging. It was about the quality of their Christian life. Was it about keeping the show on the road or bringing people to their full potential in Christ?

When they looked at the agendas of their church meetings they were struck by how much time was spent discussing the day-to-day issues of maintenance and finance. Although these remained vitally important they set themselves a new set of priorities: to renew their worship so that Jesus could be seen in it; to develop fellowship and nurture in the church; and to discover how to do evangelism. This was perhaps the hardest admission of all: that they did not know where to begin with evangelism. They thought it was something evangelicals did, and on the whole they felt rather uncomfortable about it. It conjured up images of painful encounters, knocking on the doors of strangers, or embarrassing rallies where people were exhorted to give their lives to Jesus.

They were encouraged to look at a model for evangelism which described the process as a journey and emphasised that the church needed to accompany people on the way to faith. Some of them went off on a training programme put on by the diocese, and the Diocesan Adviser with responsibility for evangelism came and spoke to the PCC and preached one Sunday. At last they began to imagine that evangelism might be something their church could engage in. This was a way of understanding evangelism which resonated with their theology and spirituality.

They also set about a painful task of liturgical renewal, and in particular there was renewed teaching about the sacraments as encounters with Jesus. Although this had a dramatic effect on the worship, it had the greatest impact in the area of fellowship. They adopted a kind of cell structure for their church in which every member was put in a fellowship group which met once a month. Even though less than half the congregation actually attended, everyone knew they were part of a group and the groups happily took on basic responsibilities for pastoral care as well as providing a forum for fellowship, prayer, Bible study and Christian teaching. Most of all it was helping many of them to pray. This more than anything was a way that Jesus could be given a face in their community.

Hitherto prayer had been something that happened in church or in situations of dire emergency. But now there was a growing desire to know God personally. The Eucharist, which remained at the heart of the church's life, was now feeling more relevant and accessible. Some members of the congregation were starting to read the Bible and using daily Bible reading notes. There was even a suggestion that there ought to be a parish retreat or week of guided prayer.

The purpose statement had spurred them into life. For the first time in a long while they felt as if they were all marching to the same tune. This did not mean that there were no disagreements. If anything there were more. The difference was that there were some agreed criteria whereby disputes could be judged. Whereas in the past disagreements had been factional, now they were tactical. It was about how they put their vision into action, rather than arguing about the different outcomes of different visions. Best of all it was discovered that people who had major disagreements with the way the church was going found themselves wrestling with God rather than the vicar!

They saw their purpose statement as a tool. Everyone in the church was given a copy, and a short planning document was produced which showed how the different elements in the statement were beginning to be shaped into a parish plan. But the vision was not static. They did not pin their statement on the wall and admire it. They put it to work in the exciting business of becoming a missionary church. Producing their purpose statement helped them realise the more fundamental truth: that God was calling *them* to be his purpose statement.

5

BUILDING A PLACE OF NURTURE

THERE IS A FANTASY ABOUT EVANGELISM: people hear the gospel, repent, and look around for a church to join. Then there is the reality: people come into contact with the church, or have some inkling of the possibility of God, and enter into a relationship with the church, either through its activities, its worship, or just friendship with its members. In the loving community of these relationships faith begins to grow. Or to put it more succinctly: belonging comes before believing. Therefore, right at the heart of any effective evangelistic ministry must be a warm and generous attitude to those who are currently outside the church community, and a place of welcome and nurture within it. Robert Warren identifies 'making room for all' as one of the seven marks of a healthy church (see also p. 8).

Nurturing a generous attitude of welcome to newcomers is something that needs to be worked at over many years. Most churches pride themselves on being friendly and welcoming. The truth is often rather different. In my first year as Diocesan Missioner in the Wakefield diocese I liked, occasionally, to turn up unannounced, and under-dressed, at a church on a Sunday morning and just observe how I was received. Very often the church was good at making me feel welcome as I came through the door, cheerily smiling as I was given a pile of books. Rarely did that welcome extend to offering any explanation as to how to navigate my way through them, nor – when I needed friendship the most – at the end of the service, did anyone consider it their job to speak to me. I was strongly encouraged to stay and drink some fairly hideous coffee, but there was no one to talk with me. They were already in their holy huddles.

Welcome is not just what we do when someone comes through the door. It is an attitude which seeks to get inside the shoes of the other person so that they can be welcomed and accompanied at every point of their journey.

By 'friendly' what most churches mean is 'friendly to each other' (we find the church friendly, because we know everyone and we know how the service works). As a test of how welcoming and friendly your church really is, ask yourself this question: if twenty or thirty new people turned up next Sunday, how would you feel? Would this really be good news? What if they sat in your seat? What if they didn't understand the service? What if they outnumbered you? What if there were changes they wanted to make?

Welcome, from a Christian standpoint, means welcoming change. To welcome someone into the church is like adopting a new member into your family.[1] You would not think of doing this without recognising the disruption and change it will bring. So it is with welcoming new people into the life of faith.

One of the chief reasons that many churches don't grow, is because they don't want to. They won't admit it, but they are not prepared to make the sacrifices and changes that will be necessary to welcome new people in. They are prepared to incorporate one or two, who 'fit in' with who they are and their way of doing church, but are not prepared to face the more radical change that is required if we are to be truly welcoming to all.

Moreover, it is likely that some of the people who will be most attracted to a church which is seeking to be truly welcoming are those who often find it most difficult to fit in elsewhere: those who have been marginalised and excluded in the rest of society. Churches of a catholic tradition have always had a wonderful tradition of welcoming the marginalised, but in recent years we have often appeared preoccupied with other issues and have seen other churches develop this sort of welcome. The fact that they are welcoming is good, but we need to recover that open spirit that counts everyone in, particularly those who feel oppressed or misunderstood.

And all this, let us remember, is because we have a God who is welcoming and inclusive. The gospel we share is one that counts people in. Therefore, before we go any further in developing a ministry of evangelism we have to face the question: do we want our church to grow? Are we prepared to face the cost? Have we truly considered what it means to be welcoming?

If the answer is yes, then we need to develop the ministry of welcome in our church by ensuring that in our worship welcome is extended at every point of the service, including what happens afterwards; and that our congregations are challenged and taught about God's generosity and welcome. We need to allow our own prejudices and inconsistencies to be challenged by a gospel that looks on everyone with love. In order to give practical expression to our desire to help people make the journey to faith we need a place where this can happen. The rest of this chapter will look at how we can create a place of nurture.

A PLACE OF NURTURE

A place of nurture can take many different forms. The most obvious, and probably the most fruitful, is some sort of enquirers' group. This is a place where people can:

• explore faith and
• experience Christian community.

Both of these are important, because the belonging and the believing go hand in hand.

Becoming a Christian is not just learning about the Christian faith: it is about becoming a member of the Christian community, and it is about relationship with a God who is himself a community of persons. Therefore, right at the beginning of the journey, people need to experience what it means to be part of a pilgrim church. Before people can become pilgrims themselves they need to feel happy to travel with us and be open to experiencing life from a Christian perspective.

The place of nurture needs to be a safe place, where people are at ease, where they can bring their questions, and where they will feel challenged, but not pressured. People need to feel comfortable: they need to feel that their questions and concerns are taken seriously.

I like to use the term 'travellers' to refer to people who are beginning to explore the Christian faith, because it describes those who are on the way. They may not yet be coming to church, but they are committed to taking the next step. For many people the best next step is a course of enquiry where they can enter into dialogue with the Christian faith in the company of other Christian people.

There are several questions that a church which wants to develop its place of nurture needs to address:

• Which course to use?
• How do the courses work?
• Who will lead it?
• Where should it happen?
• How often?
• Who will come?

We shall address these in turn.

WHICH COURSE TO USE, AND HOW DO THEY WORK?

In the past fifteen years there has been a huge development of resources to help churches in the ministry of nurture, which is also sometimes referred to as 'process evangelism'. But it is not a term I particularly like. While the whole ministry of evangelism certainly is a process, I prefer the word 'journey'. The place of nurture – and usually a nurture course – cannot be separated from the basic ministry of service, outreach and proclamation which precedes it, nor from the ongoing growth and discipleship that follows. However, the place of nurture is one of the most vital and significant points on the journey to faith and does require a particular ministry. Therefore we must ensure it is established before we attempt to develop the other aspects of a holistic ministry of evangelism. That is why I prefer to refer to these courses as nurture courses and see them as part of a whole ministry of evangelism, which is itself about helping people make the journey.

Far and away the most famous and widely used of these materials is the *Alpha* course. Developed at Holy Trinity Brompton, *Alpha* is a fifteen-session nurture course that is now used by thousands of churches worldwide. However, little recognised is the work of those who have revived the Catechumenate in churches across the world, particularly in situations of mission, such as in Africa, which was a forerunner of the modern courses. The Catechumenate was the model for evangelism, nurture and discipleship used by the early Church. Its revival in the Roman Catholic Church in the post-war period led to a revival of interest in the world-wide Anglican Communion. In the Church of England pioneers such as Peter Ball were instrumental in setting up the Catechumenate Network. The latest guide to this way of approaching evangelism and nurture is listed in the resources at the end of this chapter.

The Roman Catholic Church has been very strong on liturgical material to mark the different stages of a journey into faith, but less good on teaching materials at the very earliest stages of the journey.

The Catechumenate movement in the Church of England, learning from the insights of best educational practice, offered a different vision to the straight-line evangelistic model which was prevalent at that time. At the heart of the process was the open attitude of welcome that was given to those who enquired about faith. Inspired by the example of Jesus on the Emmaus Road, the idea was that the agenda of the meeting should be set by the questions of the enquirers. In the same way that Jesus had asked Cleopas and his companion what they were discussing as they walked along (Luke 24:17), so we should ask those who were enquiring about faith what questions they had. Consequently any suggestion of an existing agenda, or worse a curriculum, was quickly shunned. The group wrote its own agenda, starting with a blank piece of paper.

However, a new group of people gathering together for the first time, and not necessarily knowing one another, are not likely to come out straightaway with the questions that matter most. Because it takes time to get to know each other and develop trust, everything can be rather superficial to begin with. The thinking in the Catechumenate Network placed great emphasis on sharing story and building trust. These principles of starting with the questions of those who are enquiring, and building good relationships by sharing stories, still seem to me to be vitally important for the development of a healthy ministry of evangelism. However, one of the reasons that the pioneering insights of the Catechumenate Network never really took off in the Church of England was that to run a course in this way required a high degree of skill and no little nerve. Flying by the seat of your pants was obligatory. Also – and of course this is a criticism that can be levelled at most of the materials produced – it is one thing to have a really good course, it is another to get people to come on it.

But for the time being let us stick with the dynamics of the group itself. The generation of materials typified by *Alpha* and *Emmaus* has been effective because they have incorporated the principles of the Catechumenate and packaged them in an attractive way that was easy for churches to adopt. In an *Alpha* course, where the meal together is as important as the teaching, the environment the meal creates embodies welcome and hospitality and provides an atmosphere in which people feel at ease and get to know each other well. The materials, particularly the video, enable churches to present the basics of Christian faith in a fairly easy way. The discussion afterwards enables people to ask their questions.

The other course that is most widely used in the Church at the moment is *Emmaus*. Here I must declare an interest as one of its authors, but I would say it goes further than *Alpha* in that it sets out to present the ideas of the Catechumenate in a way that is much more accessible to parishes. It is a library of resources which help churches to accompany enquirers from the point of initial contact, through a fifteen-session nurture course, to ongoing growth in discipleship.

Like *Alpha*, it parts company with the Catechumenate in offering a programme of learning – a syllabus. But the educational style is different from *Alpha*. Where *Alpha* has a series of talks or videos, *Emmaus* offers a small group programme of discussion and exploration. One is not better than the other. They are different educational models. *Emmaus* tries to give greater emphasis to the idea of an accompanied journey: a group of people who are enquiring about Christian faith join with others from the local church to walk together – as if to *Emmaus* – and to explore the Christian faith. The material is arranged in such a way that there is plenty of room for personal story, for reflection and for questioning. But the hope is for dialogue. There is a creative inter-play between explaining and exploring. The basics of the Christian faith are presented through the nurture course, but in a context where there is plenty of room for questions and plenty of encouragement to abandon the prescribed agenda and go with the questions of the group.

Theological differences between *Alpha* and *Emmaus* are, in my opinion, overstated. The main differences are scope – *Emmaus* starts at an earlier stage in the journey and goes on much further – and educational method, as described above. *Emmaus* includes material on the sacraments while *Alpha* does not; but the widespread use of *Alpha* by the Roman Catholic Church should be sufficient evidence to show that as a basic exploration of the Christian faith it can happily be used by catholic parishes.

Other courses and resources for the ministry of nurture are listed and briefly evaluated at the end of this chapter. Nor should home-made resources be ignored. Research done by Mark Ireland, the missioner in the Lichfield diocese, indicates that these can be as effective, and sometimes more effective than bought resources.[2] A church that has produced its own material, perhaps has an increased commitment to making it work that can bear fruit in encouraging more people to come along. However, most churches will not have the time or the energy to produce their own material. They need to look carefully at what is available and then find the course that best suits their situation. It will then be important to adapt it, so that it really fits.

But the really important question is: are you doing anything at all? Bob Jackson, in his influential little book *Hope for the Church*,[3] notes that over half the churches in England are not. In my teaching about nurture and evangelism I liken a church without a place of nurture to a hospital without a maternity ward! No wonder there are no babies being born! It seems to me unthinkable that when there is such a body of evidence indicating the difference that a nurture course makes, churches can still do nothing about it. It needs to become a national – or at least a diocesan policy – that every church should develop a place of nurture and put on some sort of course for enquirers on a regular basis.

My basic advice is: find the course that's best for you. But, for heaven's sake, do something!

WHO WILL LEAD IT?

Many churches may feel that only the clergy are qualified to lead an enquirers' course and this may be the best way to get started. However, if the principle is established that whenever a group meets, there is at least one apprentice leader learning on the job, there is every good reason to hope that in two or three years a leadership team for this ministry will have been established. The development of such a model is not as difficult as is often imagined. The biblical model for training is apprenticeship. Too often lay people are sent off on lengthy training courses, whereas Jesus said, 'Follow me' – and learn on the job! If, at the beginning, the priest is the only person in the church ready and willing to lead a nurture course for enquirers, then from day one it will be very important to have the deputy apprentice leader in place. By going through the whole of the course once, and slowly sharing some of the responsibilities of leadership, the apprentice leader will be ready not only to lead a group, but also to apprentice another leader. This is the model we need to foster in our churches, and I have seen it work in some of the most deprived parishes of urban Britain. Missionary structures require the development of lay leadership. I also think that two people leading a group are better than one. Jesus sent his disciples out in pairs.

If you are taking the ministry of hospitality seriously, then other people, who may not be called to lead the group, can act as hosts, taking prime responsibility for welcome and refreshment, sharing the leadership in that way.

When the *Emmaus* materials were developed in West Yorkshire virtually all the groups who piloted it were lay led, having only received one evening of training. The book *Leading an Emmaus Group*[4] will be helpful whatever course you run. It explains some of the basic principles of leading a nurture group, providing just the right amount of encouragement and practical help that many lay people will need in order to get started in this ministry.

Sponsors

The ministry of hospitality to participants on the nurture course can be further extended by the provision of 'sponsors', which was an idea pioneered by the Catechumenate model. Sponsors act as companions to those who are exploring faith. They embody the welcome, care and concern of the whole Christian community. Their role is:

- to share faith
- to offer friendship
- to pray regularly.

Since it can be a little off-putting for someone who is joining a nurture group to find that they are being given a sponsor (though this does work well in some situations), I prefer to encourage a few members of the church community to act as sponsors to all those who are enquiring. This has the double advantage of modelling the nurture process as an accompanied journey, where ordinary Christian people walk alongside those who are enquiring, and helping make a viable group. In many situations there are only a few people who want to join a nurture group. With such small numbers getting the group to function well can be hard work. However, if you add two or three sponsors to the two or three enquirers and if you also have a couple of leaders and someone acting as host, you quickly find you have a group of about ten people and a meeting which is much more likely to go well.

I also prefer to sit light to the terminology. I don't usually call the people sponsors; I just say there are some members of the congregation who are joining in the process to offer friendship and share their own experiences of faith. If they are also praying for the enquirers, then not only will the groups go well, but when these people do attend church services there will be some church members they already know. This helps enormously in integrating people into the worshipping life of the church. Research indicates that one of the main factors determining whether people stick with church or not concerns whether they have made any significant relationships.[5] It is the belonging which is most important.

Both the *Emmaus* and the Catechumenate material give more information about the role of sponsors, which can include a liturgical role. Sometimes the sponsor can present the candidate at baptism or confirmation and stand alongside them.

WHERE SHOULD IT HAPPEN?

The venue rather depends on which course you are using. *Alpha* courses usually envisage a largish gathering with a meal and often happen in a hall or other similar-sized venue. *Emmaus* groups usually envisage a smaller gathering of people meeting in a home. But many *Alpha* groups happen around dining tables in people's homes, and I have known *Emmaus* groups meet in the pub, and *Youth Emmaus* groups usually meet in classrooms during lunch breaks at school. Other groups meet in the workplace or in any other kind natural meeting place. As a basic rule it is best to find a venue that is not a church building itself. Ideally you want somewhere neutral where it is easy to create a friendly and welcoming environment.

The place of nurture that is right for one group of people – say, residents in a sheltered housing block – will not necessarily be right for another – say, young parents. Often, the place of nurture arises out of the place of contact. Therefore, it is very important to be flexible and to seek to ensure that the pattern of nurture remains adaptable so that it can cross-fertilise into different situations.

So much depends on circumstances, the course you are using and the people you have invited. All the rules are there to be bent and, where necessary, broken. The friendliness of your welcome and your desire to walk with people on their journey are much more important than the course you use or the venue you occupy. Always have a low doctrine of the course itself and a high doctrine of what God can do through a welcoming and hospitable church that takes the ministry of nurture seriously.

The Rule of St Benedict can provide us with encouragement here: 'All who arrive as guests are to be welcomed like Christ, for he is going to say, "I was a stranger and you welcomed me."'[6] It might be providential for many other aspects of church life if we tested their effectiveness against the criterion of whether they have enabled us to serve Christ in the poor and the excluded. As the letter to the Hebrews reminds us: 'Let mutual love continue. Do not neglect to show hospitality to strangers, for by doing that some have entertained angels without knowing it' (Hebrews 13:1–2).

HOW OFTEN?

In the early part of a church's journey towards becoming a missionary church it will probably not be possible to run a nurture course more than once a year, because setting up and running a course makes high demands on time and leadership. Most crucially of all, there needs to be a steady flow of people wanting to come on the course! Although many churches start off by running the course with church members, for the place of nurture to do its work it will need to be attracting seekers who want to make the journey.

Another frustration is that, no matter how thorough planning for the course has been, the response of those outside the church rarely fits in with the proposed timetable. No sooner has the course started than someone appears wanting to find out more. It is not impossible to incorporate them, but it is not ideal. In time it will be possible to run more than one course each year, but this depends on building up a team of leaders and an evangelistic ministry that is bearing fruit in people seeking faith.

It is also important to bear in mind that the completion of a course is not the end of the journey. Our aim is to see travellers become pilgrims and enter into the life of the church. For some this will happen during the nurture course, but by no means all. Just as people's initial response does not fit in with our timetable, so conversion itself is usually a process over which we have no direct control. Having said this, churches are always surprised and delighted by the massive development people who seemed so far from the gospel can make in even a fifteen-week course. For those who are ready to explore faith, often the course itself can quickly bring them to a point where they wish to make a full confession of faith and be baptised or confirmed into the household of the church. For others it will happen later. And yet others will fall away. We don't want it to happen, but throughout our ministry we need always to remember that God is the Evangelist. In building a place of nurture we are creating a space where people can attend to the basic questions of life and faith. Our task is to create that space, remove the obstacles that are getting in the way of people engaging with the gospel, present the gospel as clearly as we can, and listen attentively to the concerns and questions people bring. But how they respond to what God has done in Christ is their affair.

In the Emmaus Road story we are told at the beginning that the disciples' eyes are kept from recognising Jesus (Luke 24:16). God is somehow present even in their lack of recognition, perhaps bringing them to a point where they could make a free response to all that God had done in Christ. But even when they make that free response and recognise Christ in the breaking of the bread, Luke suggests it is still God's work: 'their eyes were opened' (Luke 24:31).

Bob Jackson offers us another crucial insight. He notes that it is when churches are using courses like *Alpha* or *Emmaus* for the third or fourth time that there is some noticeable growth. As we observed, the first couple of courses often only attract church members. This is OK. Before we can ever invite anyone else along we need to find out for ourselves how it works. We also humbly recognise that our own faith needs refreshing.

However, it is at this point that many churches give up. The course has worked well, but they had unrealistic hopes about who else would join. They thought that putting on the course was enough in itself. But the nurture course is just part of the process. In order to reap the full benefit, sufficient expertise and leadership needs to be developed so that it can be run regularly – hopefully, at least once or twice a year. Although this requires a lot of work, it is necessary so that all the rest of the work can be fruitful. Having a place of nurture and running a nurture course needs to become an ordinary part of church life.

Speaking of nurture courses and the impact they have had in recent years, Bob Jackson also says, 'The job for the Church of England in the next few years is something it is not normally good at – to take what began as a fringe idea, recognise its God-given potency for sharing faith and the growth of the Church and make it thoroughly and respectably mainstream in the life of every parish.'[7] Flowing out of a renewal of the Catechumenate, this way of evangelising is so deeply rooted in the catholic tradition it seems a particular irony that most Christians think it was invented by Holy Trinity Brompton and a particular scandal that many catholic parishes do not run regular nurture courses.

WHO WILL COME?

So that there is no misunderstanding I want to reiterate again that numerical growth – or even the number of people attending courses – is not the only way, or even the best way, of indicating a church's health or faithfulness. What I am saying is that in order to be faithful we must take the ministry of nurture seriously. Through it we are expressing the hope that people will come to faith and join the church: not because we are concerned with either the survival of an institution or the building of an ecclesiastical power-base, but so that God's kingdom can be established.

Building a place of nurture is an important building block in the evangelistic ministry, tried and tested by many churches of different denominations and traditions. Once it is in place its focus needs to turn to the much harder question of accompanying people to that point on the journey where they are ready to find out more. This issue will be addressed in detail in the next chapter. But the development of a place of nurture not only provides a place of refreshment for existing church members but straightaway provides opportunities for inviting others. Once the course is advertised, and people in the congregation know it is happening, all the pastoral work that is already going on can be focused towards recruiting a group of people to begin this process of discovery.

Without doing anything else, most churches will find that there are bereaved people, baptism families, wedding couples and others who will respond positively to the invitation to find out more. In so many pastoral situations clergy and lay people find themselves dealing with people whose questions are leading them to faith. If it were possible to visit them regularly, surely they would come to faith. Sadly, this is rarely possible. It is not that all these people will respond positively to an invitation to join a nurture course. But some will. While they will usually decline an invitation to come to church on Sunday, they may welcome an opportunity to join a group of fellow travellers, Christians and other seekers, exploring what faith is about.

However, it is important to be proactive. My advice is to put dates in the diary for the course before you have any candidates. This will speak powerfully of the new priority mission is taking in the life of the church. It will also have the psychological effect of helping everyone in the church gear their thinking towards outreach.

CELEBRATIONS ON THE WAY

As churches develop the ministry of evangelism that is outlined in this book they may well find it profitable to incorporate rites into the liturgy to celebrate the awakening of faith and people's journey towards initiation. In the Church of England the Adult Catechumenate has pioneered liturgical materials, and rites have now also been produced by the Liturgical Commission.[8] They are published in *Christian Initiation* in the section 'Rites Supporting Disciples on the Way of Christ'.

The texts that have particular relevance to this book are:

- a rite of welcome for those who after an initial exploration of the Christian faith want to go the next step
- an affirmation of the Christian Way – a brief rite that could be used in many settings where those exploring faith are present
- a celebration of the decision to be baptised or confirmed or affirm baptismal faith
- prayers in preparation for baptism
- a celebration for a church to hold itself *after* an initiation service has happened elsewhere

- thanksgiving for baptism
- admission of the baptised to communion (chiefly intended for use with children where they are admitted to communion before confirmation).

The *Emmaus* materials also included liturgical material, namely:

- a service welcoming an enquirer in the Way of Christ
- a service of welcome after baptism, confirmation or affirmation of baptismal faith.[9]

As someone involved in producing these resources, my own experience of using them has been that they help incorporate those who are exploring faith into the worshipping life of the church. They do this in a way that involves the whole congregation, symbolises growth in faith and marks the steps of the journey. Some churches need a bit of encouragement to use them the first time. However, I don't know of any churches that, having used these rites once, have not used them again. Churches of a catholic and liturgical tradition will find it natural and helpful to celebrate the ministry of evangelism and nurture within the worshipping life of the community.

In Peterborough Cathedral, where I served as Canon Pastor, we made our Epiphany Carol service each year into a celebration of those who were exploring the way of faith. Using some of the rites listed above we developed a moving and beautiful liturgy whose focus was the manifesting of faith in the lives of those who were looking forward to baptism and confirmation at Easter. Advent was the time set aside for initial exploration of faith, and during Epiphanytide and Lent there was a follow-on course for those wanted to explore further. The Epiphany Carol Service, therefore, seemed an excellent opportunity to celebrate their decision to become fellow travellers in faith and seek initiation into the Church.

COURSES AND RESOURCES
I. Nurture courses
Alpha (published by Kingsway)
This famous nurture course from Holy Trinity Brompton is widely used by a huge number of churches and is very effective. In particular it places the sharing of the gospel within a social context: every *Alpha* meeting is supposed to begin with a meal. The teaching method is quite up-front – a talk or video followed by smaller discussion groups. It will not, therefore, transfer so well into small-group situations which work much better if they are based in a home and centred around discussion. Its main weaknesses from a catholic perspective are not so much what it says but what it doesn't say. *Alpha* comes from a Charismatic Evangelical background and therefore does not cover some aspects of faith that some Christians would

consider basic. There is, for instance, hardly anything about the sacraments. But having said this, quite a few catholic parishes, both Roman and Anglican, use *Alpha*.

Emmaus (published by Church House Publishing)
Emmaus is based on a Catechumenate model but still has a fifteen-session nurture course at its heart. It tries to strike a balance between explanation and exploration. It is less prescriptive than *Alpha* but not as open-ended as the Catechumenate approach. There is liturgical material – rites to mark the different stages of the journey – and information about sponsors to accompany people on the journey. *Emmaus* has three stages – Contact, Nurture and Growth – and is published in six volumes, so, unlike the other materials, starts a lot earlier in the seeker's journey of exploration and goes a lot deeper. Whichever course is used, the *Emmaus* Contact book will be of enormous benefit to churches which are wanting to think through how to get people to come on a course, as will the *Emmaus* Growth modules for following up basic instruction and exploration. Many churches which use the *Alpha* course, use *Emmaus* growth courses as part of the follow-up. The authors of *Emmaus* come from a cross-section of Christian traditions.

Both *Alpha* and *Emmaus* also publish youth versions of their nurture material.

Faith on the Way – a Practical Guide to the Adult Catechumenate (published by Continuum)
This book by Peter Ball and Malcolm Grundy provides the latest practical guide to developing evangelism and nurture using the ideas of the Catechumenate. It includes theory, practice and liturgical material.

Start! (published by the Church Pastoral Aid Society)
This is a six-session video-based introduction to the Christian faith aimed to be more accessible to a non-book culture. Its immediacy, lively presentation and less middle-class feel are all to be commended. Its brevity might also seem an advantage, though often it takes six sessions before people feel comfortable enough to raise their real questions, so *Start!* will probably work best in conjunction with something else.

Other resources to help with the work of nurture
Evangelism – which way now? An evaluation of Alpha, Emmaus, Cell church and other contemporary strategies for evangelism (published by Church House Publishing)

It does what it says on the tin! This accessible book by Mike Booker and Mark Ireland assesses and evaluates some of the main evangelism strategies of recent years, concentrating particularly on process evangelism courses.

On the Way – Towards an Integrated Approach to Christian Initiation (published by Church House Publishing)
This House of Bishops' Report encourages the development of Catechumenate thinking and promotes the link between evangelism and nurture.

Leading an Emmaus Group (published by Church House Publishing)
This is one of the books in the family of *Emmaus* material, but it is useful no matter what course a church is running since it deals with issues of leadership.

Example

Many people are scared stiff of evangelism. It is associated with coercion, manipulation, triumphalism, dogmatism and plain embarrassment. Even though the reality of how evangelism actually happens in the vast majority of churches is a million miles away from these fears, many churches still do not have evangelism on the agenda. Even those churches which have a purpose statement and a mission strategy often let evangelism sit on the back burner. Phrases like 'well, everything is evangelistic' and 'we aren't called to be evangelists' allow the church to avoid doing anything specific.

A church that wants to move forward in its evangelistic ministry needs to teach its members, and especially those in lay leadership, how evangelism works for most people. The model for evangelism we are looking at here and the aims which flow from it, also need to be presented and understood.

One of the best ways of doing this is to ask your PCC or your congregation to reflect on the story of their own faith. You can conduct your own piece of research. Get people to tell each other how they came to faith and then ask them to put themselves into categories, working out who had dramatic Damascus-Road-type experiences – there will be some – and who had gradual Emmaus-Road-type experiences – this will be the vast majority.

Once people realise that there is a new way of understanding evangelism, it is relatively easy to start developing the structures and ministries in the church that can enable progress to be made.

Insight gained from the Decade of Evangelism has resulted in seeing evangelism as the sharing of spirituality as a way of life as well as the communication of doctrinal truth. It is not insignificant that the primary documents of the Christian Church are *stories* of faith. Christian people in the day-to-day task of evangelism should be sharing two beautiful and unique stories: the story of what God has done in Jesus Christ and the story of what God has done in their own life.

In the case of St Mary's, the church's purpose statement clearly identified evangelism as part of their missionary task. They wanted members of their community to find their full potential as children of God. But they did not really know how to make this happen.

Encouraged by the training event on evangelism that some members of the church had attended, at a PCC meeting everyone present was encouraged to share with their neighbour their own story of faith. When these stories were analysed it turned out that of the fourteen people present only two had had a dramatic conversion experience. All the others told stories of gradually coming to faith. For some it was only when they looked back that they realised they had become a Christian. Many had come to church since infancy. For them it was important to share the story of when their faith became real, or the story of how they had lapsed and returned to faith. For most of the PCC it was the first time they had ever told anyone about their own faith story.

From this exercise it was easy to demonstrate some of the basic truths about evangelism:

1. *You can't give what you haven't got.* Somewhere along the line everyone had been impressed and impacted by someone whose faith was real.
2. *Coming to faith is more like a journey than an event.* Nearly everyone told a story of gradually coming to faith. When the diagram relating to contact, nurture, commitment, church membership and growth was shown (see p. 40), people were readily able to remember these different phases of their own spiritual growth.
3. *The best sort of evangelism is the Christlike witness of ordinary Christians.* The key factors leading to faith nearly always involved family members, close friends or the ministry of the church in the wider community.
4. *Belonging comes before believing.* Everyone spoke of the importance of being welcomed into the life of the church; of fellowship; of a church that was able to accompany people on the journey from interested unbelief to committed faith.

As a church they could now see several priorities for the way they were being called to work: evangelism must become a continual dimension in the whole life of the church, not just an occasional activity. The church was not supposed to have a mission, it was supposed to *be a mission*. This would mean placing an even higher priority on deepening the faith of those who already came to church so that they could grow into an apostolic faith. It would also mean setting up structures for nurture and looking creatively at how they could use the contacts they already had. It would also mean making new contacts. As they explored this approach to evangelism it became clear that most of the PCC knew very few people outside the church. The business of running the church had voraciously consumed most of their time and energy, so that contacts with non-Christians were almost non-existent. Not only did they realise how important it was to develop in themselves a sense of their own responsibility for carrying forward God's mission, they also saw the need to streamline church structures. Room needed to be made for new initiatives in the areas of contact and nurture. Space needed to be found so that committed church people could develop friendships and relationships outside of church life. As they began to do this, so they also began to build the structures that would enable people to discover faith. First of all they needed to develop a place of nurture.

They decided to run an *Emmaus* nurture course once a year. It was then early summer and they put the dates in the diary for it to begin on the week following Advent Sunday. This wasn't a great time for newcomers – the build-up to Christmas – but they liked the idea of a fresh start at the beginning of the Church's year. It also gave them enough time to begin inviting people to come, and the hope that one or two might say yes. Everyone felt very apprehensive. There was a lot of disagreement about whether anyone would come; about whether they should spend more time deepening their own faith before they tried to share it with others; about who would lead the groups; about where they should take place. Eventually they decided that they could spend forever waiting to be ready and it was much better just to begin.

The first course would be led by their priest with two apprentice leaders. The group would meet in the home of one of the lay leaders and, if the numbers grew, in the church hall (not ideal, but there was nowhere else in the parish). Anyway, they did not think large numbers would be their problem. They were fearful that no one would come and, for this reason if no other, they decided each person who came as an enquirer would be given a sponsor. They had read about the role of a sponsor and liked the idea of someone having a ministry of companionship towards the person who was seeking. Best of all they thought it would help make a viable group if only one or two signed up.

All this was done with great trepidation, frequent squabbles, and much looking over the shoulder wondering why they had ever started down this particular road. Setting up the place of nurture was hard work – made harder because it was difficult to see how it would bear fruit. It was also hard because in a small church most of the committed members already had other jobs. This meant that there were certain things they had to stop doing. They took the big risk of cancelling their summer fete. It never made that much money anyway, but they felt it was more important to free up some of their time so that they could concentrate on what was really important. So they persevered. All the evidence from other churches and from what they had read encouraged them to believe that this could not be a quick-fix. It was like building a maternity ward in the church. A new ministry was being developed and it took time and effort. But in time they found they could begin to think about how to invite others to come and explore faith with them, and this, of course, felt harder still!

6

GETTING STARTED/DEVELOPING CONTACT

W E NOW TAKE A STEP BACKWARDS to examine what is undoubtedly the hardest part of evangelism – the first part – developing contact with people on the fringes of the church or outside the Christian community altogether.

There is some good news, however. Every church is in contact with hundreds of people. Mostly this is through our daily lives as Christians – our friends, family, colleagues and neighbours. This list alone runs into hundreds. Then there are the groups of people with whom we have contact through the ministry of the church – the bereaved; those who come to us for baptisms and weddings; uniformed organisations; church hall users; social groups and all kinds of people. The question is: how do we use these contacts creatively so that people begin the journey to faith?

Take a standard funeral visit. Many clergy find that the bereaved person is asking questions of the nature of life and death – the very questions that might begin a journey to faith if only there were enough time to visit the person regularly and help him or her explore them. But this isn't possible, because there is another funeral tomorrow, and two more next week, and two the week after that. It is hard enough to visit before and after each of these funerals, let alone make a whole string of visits. Consequently, the person is prayed for, offered to God and forgotten about in the busyness of parish life. People are invited to come to church, but they rarely show up. Even when they do, one is painfully aware of how difficult it is for them to make sense of the liturgy. Arriving cold for the first time, and with hardly any previous contact with the Church, we are a hard institution to join, however welcoming we make ourselves. The journey to faith seems to end before it has started.

Inviting someone to a nurture group can be a more effective strategy, but even this won't necessarily work for the person who has little experience of the church and hardly any knowledge of the Christian faith. Having a lay ministry team for visiting makes an enormous difference, but there are still severe limitations on how much time can be given to one-to-one ministry of this kind. In terms of the spiritual life, if the person does not progress fairly quickly towards a point where he or she feels quite motivated to join the church, the opportunity is lost. And where one cannot establish the sort of one-to-one relationship that would really make a difference, and where there is no nurture group in place, it is 'come to church' or nothing. Although some churches make a lot of the evangelistic opportunities afforded by the Occasional Offices (and we can all point to the one or two successes of these encounters), in practice this 'come to church' kind of pastoral evangelism is little different from the 'come and be saved' of a more campaigning style. Neither has much to offer the person who needs to make a gradual journey. Before someone will come to church, and before they will even attend a nurture group, another sort of ministry is required.

ASKING THE RIGHT QUESTIONS

We need to stop starting with the church. If our strategy for evangelism begins with the question 'How can we get more people to come to church?' it is probably doomed to failure. Even if it starts with 'How can we get more people to come on our *Alpha* or *Emmaus* course?' it is probably equally doomed. We need to start with people: the people with whom we have contact and the issues they are facing in their lives. We can then build stepping stones towards the place of nurture and the worshipping life of the Christian community.

We have already noted that belonging comes before believing. Well, before belonging comes blessing. Here is a question around which the church could usefully develop its evangelism:

> **How can we serve the people with whom we have contact in such a way that the gospel is intriguing, challenging and appealing?**

Although it is not a very snappy question, it asks us to consider how we can be a blessing to our local community, and it is carefully honed to get us to the heart of evangelistic ministry.

It doesn't ask, 'How can we *convert* the people with whom we have contact?', but 'How can we *serve* them?' The first message of the gospel must be one of loving service. How can we bless people? It speaks of the people *with whom we already have contact.* There are plenty of people we don't have contact with, but hundreds that we do.

The first practical step towards developing an evangelistic ministry is to list these groups of people. And I do mean actually make a list. This can be done with a mission planning group, or at the PCC. On a large piece of paper you write down the 'people groups' that your church has contact with. By 'people group' I mean the groups we referred to earlier – husbands who don't come to church; flower arrangers; parents and toddlers; hall users, etc. But of course every group of people is made up of individuals. As we do this exercise for real, because we are thinking of people with whom we already have contact, we will be listing groups, but thinking of individuals: individuals we know and whom God loves.

At this point in the process resist thinking about what you are going to do with them. Just list the groups of people. The age-old problem for the church is that we often put events before people. We then try to fit people into our agenda and our activities. Some social or evangelistic event will be planned (because someone heard that such and such a thing had been effective in another parish), and the congregation is exhorted to invite their friends to this event. Nine times out of ten, come the event, the congregation gather, but hardly anyone has brought a friend. I am often invited to speak at these sorts of events. At the post-mortem afterwards (and I use the phrase advisedly), the parish priest tells me what a rotten lot his congregation are, because they didn't invite anyone along. After a few years of hearing this I plucked up the courage to ask the priest whether he had invited anyone. I am yet to meet the clergy person who could answer in the affirmative.

In other words it is the strategy that is wrong. If you start with an event and then try to squeeze people into it, it won't usually work. You need to start with people and see where you are led. The question then is, 'How can we *serve* these people?' This is another occasion where the Emmaus Road story is of relevance. As we discussed in the last chapter, on the Emmaus Road Jesus asks Cleopas and his companion, 'What are you discussing together as you walk along?' (Luke 24:17 NIV). We spoke about this as a starting point for the process of nurture. It can also be the starting point for evangelism in the community. In our imaginations we need to ask the same question of the groups of people we have listed and the individuals with whom we have contact. What are the questions they are asking in their life? What are the issues they are facing? What are their interests and passions? What is going on in their lives?

Having listed the groups of people, they can then be taken one at a time, and on a second piece of paper you can list their issues and interests.

To explain more clearly what I mean, let us imagine that a church has written down 'parents of school-age children' as a group with whom it has contact. As well as through the individual contacts of church members, some of whom are parents themselves, these may be contacts through a church school, or a parent and toddler group, for example.

The group then begins to think about the issues that parents face, writing another list which contains phrases like: peer pressure, money, how to be a good parent, values, dealing with awkward questions, etc.

This process is easy and enjoyable. These are people we know, and in many cases we are facing the same issues ourselves: we have contact with this group of people because at least some of us are part of that group. We are not writing down groups of people we would *like* to have contact with, but ones where there is *already* some real relationship.

With some groups it will be more appropriate to think about the interests that unite them rather than the issues they face. But with each group we ask what I call 'the Emmaus Road question', 'What are these people discussing as they walk along?', which we interpret in our situation as meaning, 'What is going on in these people's lives as they make their journey through life?'

We then consider what the gospel has to say to them. It is tempting to think this is the easiest part of the process. It can often be the hardest. We either assume the answer and move swiftly on, or neglect to ask the question at all. The given-ness of the gospel leads us to think that what we say must be the same for everyone: Christ died for us and, setting us free from sin and death, offers us a new life. Of course this is true, but if we remember that for most people becoming a Christian is like a journey, we must also avoid confusing the defining relationship with God that is the journey's end, with the very particular introduction to the way of faith that may be its best beginning. In other words we need to ask ourselves what particular *aspect* of the gospel story is most likely to connect with the questions and issues this group of people or this individual is facing? Here it is helpful to let go of thinking about the Christian faith as a package deal that is simply delivered, and think of it as the beautiful and multi-faceted jewel I mentioned earlier. The question then becomes: 'Which facet of the jewel is most likely to shine brightly and directly into this person's life to illuminate it and begin to show the path he/she should follow?' Indeed, using the image of Christ having many faces, we could ask which face of Christ does this person need to see? Or thinking of the whole panoply of Scripture, which word, or which particular story, is most going to connect with this person's life? These are the right sort of questions to be asking.

On another piece of paper we begin to write down what is good news for this group of people. We remind and reassure ourselves that we have a gospel to share. We recognise that we will be unlikely to share it all at once – and we still don't know how we will share it – but we discern that there is an entry point for the journey where the issues and interests of this person's life connect with a gospel that is about the whole of life.

We need to take time on this part of the process. It is called theology, and the local church doesn't do enough of it. And, of course, it can be illuminating for our own understanding of the gospel. We remember that it is the intellectual credibility of the faith that is one of the hallmarks of effective evangelism.

We also remember our original question: the gospel should be *intriguing, challenging and appealing*. We are not just trying to find out how to attract people: we are not tailoring the gospel to suit their interests or needs. The gospel should intrigue – there will always be something delightfully inexplicable about it, leading us to want to find out more. The gospel will be challenging, making us ask hard questions about the way we live our lives. The gospel will be appealing, resonating with the deepest longings of our hearts.

With parents of young children this gospel might be the good news that Jesus himself shared the life of an earthly home, and that Mary and Joseph wrestled with all the challenges and responsibilities of parenthood in the same way we do. It might be something to do with values: many parents nowadays are concerned to bring up their children with a set of values that will equip them for life. Isn't this why so many parents want their children to go to church schools? It isn't just that educational standards appear to be higher; it is the moral and ethical framework that challenges and appeals.

Finally, when all this is done – and the process to this point will take at least an hour – we ask, 'Is there something we could do that would gather this group of people together, address in a practical way the issues and interest of their lives, and begin to communicate something of the gospel?'

Before outlining some of the principles that go into putting on an event of this kind, let me tell the stories of how several different churches have answered this question. But first a health warning: the trouble with stories like these is that they too easily become the good ideas that we suddenly think we should duplicate ourselves, thus breaking the vital rule of starting with people not events. These stories are helpful not because they enable us to bypass the process but because they illustrate how the process works!

SOME STORIES

A rural church in Staffordshire put on an evening for parents called 'Questions children ask'. Once you have heard the title you can half-guess what happened at the event. The congregation in this church included a number of young families; there was also a church school in the village. Therefore, when they went through the process I outline above, 'parents' was on their list of contacts. Many of the parents who went to church had good contact with parents at the school who didn't yet go to church, or who were on the fringes of church life. When it came to identifying the issues that concerned parents, they discovered that parenting – and in particular the difficult questions children ask on all sorts of moral and social issues – was something they kept coming back to. Many parents –

including those who were part of the planning group – observed how few opportunities there were to come together with other parents and simply talk about the job. As has often been said: being a parent is one of the most important jobs we do, yet it is the one for which we receive the least training. They also identified good news from the Christian tradition which helped give perspective on all the big questions we face in life and a moral framework for living. Out of these discussions the idea for an event emerged. What actually happened was that tickets were made and parents were invited to an evening at the school – a familiar but neutral venue where it was hoped people would feel at ease. Refreshments were served and, while people were eating and drinking, they were each given a piece of paper on which was written, 'The question I most fear being asked by my children is…'. They were then invited to fill in the blanks. The questions were then collected together and, after the refreshments were finished, everyone sat down and, one at a time, the questions were pulled from a hat and discussed. There wasn't an 'expert' up the front giving the answers; everyone was free to chip in with their own reflections and insights. Some of the questions were on moral or social issues, ranging from sex before marriage and recreational drugs to body piercing and the wearing of school uniform. There were also some questions on God. One woman said that the question she most feared being asked by her seven-year-old daughter was what happened to her grandmother when she died. And, of course, the reason that she particularly feared this question was because she didn't know how to answer it for herself. At this point one of the Christian parents in the room was able to give gentle testimony to her own faith, not telling the woman what to say, but saying what she believed about death and what she shared with her own children.

The Christian faith did not get an easy platform. Anyone in the room was free to give a different viewpoint. But on all the questions it was possible to give a Christian perspective, demonstrating that the Christian faith is concerned with the whole of life, and on some of the questions there was opportunity to give a specifically Christian answer, though often this came through the personal testimony of someone in the group, explaining how they approached that issue.

It wasn't a large gathering. About twenty parents came to the evening. The organisers were interested to observe that people tended to come in groups. There was safety in numbers. But they also found that it wasn't embarrassing to invite people. So often with evangelistic events the cringe factor is uncomfortably high. It isn't only that people don't come to the event, often they aren't even invited. With this event – because it resonated so precisely with the actual issues being faced by a group of people church members already knew well – it just wasn't embarrassing or difficult to ask them along. They knew it was being organised by the church – there was no subterfuge – but it felt like a natural and helpful thing to go along to.

At the end of the evening, having thanked people for coming and explained this was a bit of a one-off, it also felt natural to say that if anyone wanted to find out more about the Christian faith and explore life from a Christian perspective, then there were opportunities at their church to find out more. A simple feedback/response form was handed round so that people had a chance to say what they made of the evening. There was also an opportunity to indicate whether they would like to find out more about the Christian faith, or more about being a better parent. If these boxes were ticked, then there was a next step in place. Of the twenty who came to that evening, three people indicated there and then that they would like to find out more about the Christian faith. They signed up to join an *Emmaus* group and so proceeded on the journey to faith.[1]

In Pangbourne in Berkshire a similar evening was put on for parents of teenagers, inviting contacts through the church's thriving little youth group. At this event, after an excellent dinner, a speaker – who also had teenage children – spoke about the delights and challenges of sharing your life with adolescents. This was followed by questions and, again, at the end of the evening, people were asked whether they wanted to find out more and take the next step. A few said yes, but on this occasion, the evening itself was so successful that many of the parents, half of whom were not part of the local church, were very keen to meet again and discuss some of these issues. Their journey continued in another way.

In Boston in Lincolnshire a church put on an evening focusing on how Christ is represented in art. One member of the church planning group also belonged to a local art group. Her fellow members were her best contacts, which made the exercise of listing contacts very straightforward. Using slides and reproductions an imaginative evening was put together, attended by many who were not part of the church. Moreover, the art club was eager to help organise the event: this was because their own interests and endeavours were being valued.

In High Wycombe in Buckinghamshire an event was organised for the book club group to which two members of the church belonged. A book which raised spiritual questions was read and discussed by the whole group. This church also put on a fabulously creative evening of music, poems and readings reflecting the spiritual search in which many of them were engaged. I attended this evening with a student training for ordained ministry. Afterwards he commented on what a pity it was that such a challenging evening had only been attended by churchgoers. How wrong he was: most of the people there had been on the fringe or complete outsiders, but the way the evening had been organised meant that everyone was able to bring to the event a piece of music, a picture or a reading that spoke to their own sense of who God is. We had all been challenged and refined by each other's insights and questions.

In Peterborough Cathedral, where the Head of Adult Education is a member of the congregation, a course was run on Christian prayer and meditation as part of the local programme of adult education.

In Standish in Lancashire a church invited all those who had been married in the past fifty years to come back and renew their wedding vows at a mass service.

In Yorkshire a church held a huge party for all those who had been baptised in the past five years. There was a short service on a Sunday afternoon affirming baptismal faith, and then a children's party with clowns and entertainment, games, food and drink. Over 100 people attended.

A London church put on an evening called 'Stress, Stress, Stress', at which a secular speaker talked about stress management and a church member talked about prayer and meditation. Refreshments were also provided as another way of helping people off-load their worries.

In Windsor a church invited parents of children beginning at the church school to come to an evening in which the Christian ethos underpinning the life of the school was explained and commended and the life of the school introduced.

There is so much that can be done if we get the doing of it round the right way. It is called evangelism.

We start with people and we ask how we can serve them. We don't look for any particular reward other than the joy that comes from being faithful to our Lord's commission to love our neighbour and to make disciples. These two injunctions, which often seem to contradict each other (and often seem to be misinterpreted as, 'I'll love you if you come to church or if you are a Christian'), are united in this approach to evangelistic ministry. We share the gospel by our service, and we include within our service specific reference to the faith we follow. We thereby serve the whole person: their spiritual, physical, social and intellectual needs.

A HEALTH WARNING

Just like a computer, the church has a default setting, and we need to watch out that we don't revert back to it. It is all too easy to slip back into an old-style evangelism, which is just inviting people to church events and preaching at them. Or we end up just organising social events which have no gospel challenge and don't connect with the issues people are facing in life. There is nothing wrong with either of these two approaches. Social events and all that they do to build community and invite people into relationship with the church are a vitally important thing to be doing. Similarly, there is still a very important place on the journey for the basic challenge of the gospel to be laid before people with some sort of response expected. It's just that this is not what we are planning here. The approach to evangelism I am suggesting is very specific, and following this particular pattern can open doors of opportunity for the gospel. These stories simply tell what some churches have done and how small-scale do-it-yourself evangelistic events can become part of the everyday life of the local church.

The other point to note is that, in many of these stories, as well as bringing people from the church together with the people they were trying to reach, the events themselves were the fruits of some genuine collaborative effort. In other words, it wasn't the church putting on an event for people and hoping they would come. Rather, having identified the group of people and the issues they faced, the church sat down with them and the event was worked out together, thus eliminating from the very beginning the whole embarrassing question of invitation. This won't always be possible, but where it is, it seems to model something healthy and positive about the church's relationship with the wider community. It builds confidence that we have something worth sharing and fosters humility in wanting to do this alongside others from whom we can learn.

HELPING PEOPLE TAKE THE NEXT STEP

There are thousands of people growing up in Britain today who would like to find out more about the Christian faith. Some of them have reached that stage of the journey where they are ready to come to church – these are the people who find their way into the worshipping life of the church year by year. (This is good, but they are few in number.) There are more people who have reached a stage on the journey where they are ready to explore the claims of faith through a course. (This is why nurture courses like *Alpha* and *Emmaus* have been so hugely successful in recent years, and why building a place of nurture is such a vital part of the evangelistic process.)

However, the majority of people are further back down the road. They are not atheists. All the surveys of recent years show that most people have some sort of belief in God and other evidence in our culture also indicates a growing interest in spiritual things.[2] Many people have never had the opportunity to engage with issues of faith or hear the gospel presented in a way that connects with the issues they are facing in their own lives. When they do, there is a resonance: the longing of the human heart stirs in harmony with the longing of God.

The evangelising church seeks to create an environment where this can begin to happen. For many of those who are on the journey, the next step will be to join a nurture group. But often some sort of stepping stone will be needed to help them get to this stage. This is what the evangelistic event can achieve.

At every event where the gospel is being shared there should be a clearly signposted next step. This could be:

• another similar event
• an invitation to explore faith more seriously by joining a nurture course
• a visit from someone to talk about matters of faith.

We need to understand that many people find it difficult to give voice to an awakening of faith. They feel embarrassed about saying they have been moved by what has been said and unsure about what the next step should be. For this reason it is very important to give simple practical help.

One of the best ways of handling this part of the process is through a response card (see the example on p. 72). At most evangelistic events a card like this will be extremely useful, giving the reticent and the hesitant (i.e. most people!) the chance to make a response. And because the cards are handed out to everyone, no one feels singled out, and everyone, no matter where they are on the journey, has the chance to say how they feel and whether they would like to find out more. In my experience this is the best and simplest way of helping people indicate their desire to make the next step. The card can also provide other useful information for developing an evangelistic ministry. And, of course, no one has to fill it in.

A certain lightness of touch is required in introducing this part of the event. Everyone usually moans at having to fill in a dreaded evaluation sheet. But if it is kept short and simple, and if the opportunity to express interest in exploring faith is explained, hundreds of people have found it a helpful way to begin their journey to Christ. By hundreds, I do not mean hundreds at one event, but twos and threes and fours at lots of small events over a period of time as churches begin to weave this way of doing evangelism into the tapestry of church life. And for the people who respond it is a hugely significant step they are taking. Perhaps for the first time in their life they are expressing a desire to know God, or at least a desire to find out about God. And if we don't give people the opportunity to make this response then the journey to faith will be all the harder.

Usually the only thing getting in the way is our own embarrassment. Perhaps we need to remember that God is the Lover and the people at these events are the beloved whom he seeks. Christ died for these people as a demonstration of God's love and in order to create a way to life. Moreover, the peace and hope they long for can only find true satisfaction with the God who is the author of peace and the guarantor of hope. It is not our job to persuade them of the truths of this faith – someone else might come along tomorrow and persuade them something else – nor try and convert them ourselves, but we must point the way to Christ, humbly offering the opportunity to take the next step.

St Mary's, Hightown

Thank you for coming this evening. We hope you have found it an enjoyable and stimulating time.

You can help us by answering these questions. Please put a circle around the answer nearest to how you feel.

Did you enjoy this evening?

(a) A lot   (b) A little   (c) Not really   (d) Not at all

What did you like best/least?

_____

Do you think the church ought to do more of this sort of thing?

(a) Yes, definitely   (b) Yes, but not like this   (c) No

Any suggestions?

_____

Would you like to find out more about the Christian faith?

(a) Yes   (b) I'm not sure, but I would like to talk to someone about it.   (c) No

What are the particular things you want to find out about?

_____

Name _____

Address _____

_____

Tel. No. _____

Email _____

It is through this way of doing evangelism that we will find people coming onto nurture courses, and in some instances coming straight into the life of the church. In other situations people will go from one event to another similar event, or even to another sort of course. Some churches are offering courses in parenting or spirituality and finding people wanting to attend.

Visiting is also vitally important. If, as part of the preparation for the event, a team of people can be recruited who are willing to visit those who have made a response, then this, more than anything, will give clear expression of the church's loving concern.

Quite recently I was speaking at a small evangelistic event that was organised as part of a parent and toddler group meeting. After the usual activities the children were looked after while I addressed the parents, talking mainly about how they might pray with their children. Afterwards a young mum came up to me; she had been hovering on the edge of faith all her life, looking with envious eyes upon those who believed and thinking you could only really be part of the church if you could sign on the dotted line of all we held true. She was holding the response card she had been invited to fill in, but she was still unsure about taking the next step. 'The trouble is, I don't really know what I believe,' she said to me. 'I'd like to believe, but I've got so many questions.'

I gently explained that the groups the church was putting on were precisely for people like her: for people who didn't go to church and who didn't know what they believed. It was a chance to find out. At last, for her, the penny dropped. She realised that the church could be a place for seekers and fellow travellers; that it was OK to travel with the church and find out without yet believing; that we were all on a journey and all of us carried with us different questions and doubts. Indeed, the very word 'faith' includes within it the presupposition that we have questions. It is concerned with our trust not our certainty. And if the church could be trusted – if we could be that safe place where people's questions are taken seriously, and the issues of their lives addressed – then this was a place where she could begin to make her journey. She filled in the card. She decided to join an enquirers' group.

This moment of response, of reaching out, echoes another important moment in the Emmaus Road story. After Jesus has asked the two companions what they are discussing, they begin a conversation about how the Messiah was destined to suffer and die. When they arrive at Emmaus, evening is falling and Jesus makes as if to go on. 'Stay with us,' they say (Luke 24:29). These words are very significant. At this moment in the story they still don't know that it is Jesus they are talking to, and yet they ask him to stay with them. Why? Well, surely it is because he is good to be with. He has listened to their questions. He has had something worthwhile to say. The two go together: the words of Jesus flow from his attentive listening. He is listening to the people themselves and he is listening to God. Therefore he has discerned what is preventing them from recognising what God has done by raising him to life. Even though they have all the information they need to make this connection, their eyes are still closed. He is able to speak precisely into their situation uncovering for them a whole new way of understanding Scripture and a very different interpretation of what it means to be Messiah. His words had intrigue, challenge and appeal. What could be more natural than to invite him to supper?

We also need to be open to these moments of tentative response. Even if people have not yet made all the connections, and not yet made a real response to God, they have discovered enough to know that the church cares for them, takes them seriously, values their questions. They want to find out more.

Most people working in evangelism today will bear witness to the fact that this is the most common response to any sort of evangelising ministry. It is similar to the response Paul encountered when he preached the gospel in Athens – the first time he found himself in a completely alien culture. From the account in Acts 17 it is clear that some of those who heard him scoffed, some wanted to find out more and some joined him (vv. 32-4). Our ministry will have similar results. But, above all, we need to become a church that is able to help people find out more. This is the ministry of nurture that we explored in the last chapter. As we develop this kind of evangelism, so we will see it bear fruit in people wanting to find out more and travelling with us on the way to faith.

The evangelistic events described in this chapter and, more importantly, the process of discernment that leads up to them, are based upon several important principles:

1. Ask the right questions. Not, 'How can we get more people to come to church?', but 'How can we serve the people with whom we have contact in such a way that the gospel is intriguing, challenging and appealing?'
2. Let the event fit the people, not the people the event.
3. Make sure there is a next step in place.
4. Make sure the event itself deals directly with the issues and interests that the people with whom you are in contact are addressing.
5. Make sure the event expresses some aspect of the gospel.

Looking again at the model for evangelism we are exploring we can see these events act as stepping stones between initial contact and the place of nurture:

Figure 7

Here is a summary of the practical steps you need to take in order to put on such an event:

1. List the 'people groups' with whom you have contact.
2. Selecting one or two groups list their interests and the issues they face.
3. List aspects of the gospel that speak to this group of people and their issues.
4. Think of an event at which you could gather this group of people together and, as a way of serving them, begin to address the issues and share something of the gospel.
5. Work out all the practical arrangements for putting on this event, as far as possible collaborating with the people you are inviting so it is their event as much as yours.
6. Produce a response sheet and decide how you are going to use it.
7. Make sure there is a next step in place.

In churches where this strategy has worked well, there has usually been a planning group or mission team taking responsibility for developing evangelism in the parish. The steps described above do not, however, take a long time. After just a couple of meetings you can get to the point where you are actually doing something in evangelism. Setting up the place of nurture takes longer, but once that is beginning to be established, then the best next step is to get straight on with some actual evangelism. All the issues that you will face (which are so tempting to keep at arm's length) will come into sharp focus when you actually contemplate sharing faith with some real people in the way this chapter describes. But it is a marvellously fulfilling and enjoyable ministry. With the cringe factor removed, this is a catholic way of approaching evangelism that can be adopted and adapted by all Christians.

Once you have established a place of nurture, and are developing contacts in the ways explained above, the church is well on the way to getting evangelism into the bloodstream of church life.

This chapter concludes with two other elements that can be part of a parish evangelism strategy. Both begin where people are with contacts that are on our doorstep. The first is visiting – that dreaded *bête noire* of evangelism; the second is through establishing relationships with those who come to church for the Occasional Offices.

DOOR-TO-DOOR VISITING

Some parishes take a few streets each month and deliver, by hand, a copy of their parish magazine. Others audit the parish by knocking on doors, asking what people feel about local issues and how the church might help, sometimes using a questionnaire they have devised. In both of these cases the church is operating in servant mode. The emphasis is on how the church can help, rather than what the church wants.

Although it takes a bit of courage to go door-to-door visiting, and in some parts of the country electric gates can make access difficult, parishes who do it are often surprised by the good response they get, providing it is approached in the right way. At the very least it shows the church is interested in people and wants to listen to them. Many people comment on how nice it is that someone from the church has taken the trouble to call. It is always useful to take some sort of Christian literature with you.

One of the most effective ways of visiting door to door is prayer visiting. Here the church knocks on doors in the neighbourhood and asks people if there is anything they would like prayed for. You simply say, 'Hello, I'm from the local church. We feel we've lost contact a bit with many people in our parish. One of the things we can do for people is pray for them. Is there anything or anybody, you would like us to pray for?' And then see what happens next.

This sort of visiting usually meets with an extremely positive response and a huge harvest of prayer is gathered in.

When visiting door to door I have found that, while it is helpful to go out as a small team, when it comes to knocking on a door, it is better to work on your own. Not only does it make it very obvious that you are not Jehovah's Witnesses, who always go in pairs, but it is much more likely to put the person answering the door at their ease. When you knock on the door as a pair, you have the advantage. Most people answer the door on their own, so it is two against one. By knocking on the door on your own, you are the vulnerable one, and this makes initial conversation much more likely. As long as you keep sight of the others in your team and work together you will still be safe.

Of course, it is important to keep a note of people's prayer requests and to make sure the prayers are offered.

I remember prayer visiting as part of a parish mission and knocking on the door of a heavily pregnant young woman. When I asked if there was anything she would like us to pray for, she clutched her stomach and asked if I would pray for her baby who was already a week overdue. I promised we would pray, and actually took the risk of asking whether she would like me to pray with her there and then. 'Yes, please,' she said, and I prayed with her on her doorstep. This was a moving and worthwhile ministry in itself. But when I got back to the vicarage I told the parish priest where this lady lived and suggested that if he waited a few days and popped round with a bunch of flowers, saying we had been praying for her at the church and asking how things were going, we could develop what seemed a very promising contact.

When I was a parish priest we aimed to knock on every door of our parish in this way once each year as part of our ongoing evangelism strategy. People from St Catherine's Church in Tilehurst prayer visit around the parish most Friday mornings for an hour.

Door-to-door visiting also creates fresh contact with those who have lapsed from faith. A recent piece of research demonstrated that one of the main reasons people leave church is because they move house.[3] It is not that they intend to lapse, but simply fail to make contact with their local church, or having made contact fail to establish good relations with people in the church community.

Large numbers of people have left our churches over the past twenty or thirty years. Knock on the door of almost any street and you will meet one of them. In my experience a personal visit to their home is one of the ways that they may receive a nudge back towards the life of the church.

THE OCCASIONAL OFFICES

Although I sometimes think clergy place too much hope in what can be achieved through ministering to those who come to us for what are called the Occasional Offices – baptisms, weddings and funerals – they do represent wonderful opportunities to share and commend faith. Churches that take seriously their responsibilities to prepare people for baptism or for marriage – often doing it in small groups of would-be married couples or parents with newborn babies meeting together – discover that not only is the preparation good in itself but it acts as a very natural stepping stone into a nurture course. This strategy is working very effectively in Easthampstead where at a recent Confirmation there was quite a large group of young adults, most of whom had come to faith through this route. With funerals there is also opportunity for bereavement groups and bereavement visiting to act as a stepping stone, though with bereaved people it will be the quality of our care that will make the biggest difference.

Some churches also send out cards to mark the anniversary of a baptism, wedding or funeral. As well as being a sign that the church prays and remembers, it offers another opportunity for people to take a next step. If the card is accompanied by a visit, then it is all the more effective.

As we shall see in a later chapter there are also opportunities through worship to build on the contacts we have established through the Occasional Offices. Some churches hold services for the renewal of wedding vows or baptismal promises. Inviting the bereaved to come to church for All Souls' Day is another way of both reaching out and ministering to those beginning the journey.

The evangelistic effectiveness of this ministry requires that the individual baptism, wedding or funeral is part of a strategic whole with preparation beforehand and next steps to take.

Example

In September and October St Mary's held two outreach events to help encourage some of the people with whom they had contact to make the next step. They had an enjoyable evening thinking about the people groups they had contact with and then working through the process that looked at their interests and issues and how the gospel might be shared. They felt that their ideas were not as imaginative as others they had read about, but at least they had come up with them themselves and they felt a commitment to the events they began to plan. This was a way that they could help the people they knew.

They held a breakfast in the church hall for people who might be facing problems balancing the sometimes conflicting demands of home and work. They thought it was a subject that would be helpful to people outside of the church who they knew were often struggling to maintain a good balance in this area of their lives. As many of the women who came to church regularly had husbands who didn't, and for whom balancing the demands of work and home was an issue, they felt reasonably confident that they could invite them along and they would come. They also thought it would appeal to other neighbours and friends who were leading busy and pressured lives and whose families and home life were bearing the

brunt. It was also a subject many of them were concerned about. By holding it on a Saturday morning over breakfast they hoped they wouldn't be
contributing to the problem!

The event began at 9.00 and would be all over by 10.30 leaving the rest
of Saturday free.

Twenty-two people from the church community brought between them
nine non-church friends. A few of these were husbands from the first
target group. The others were a collection of acquaintances and friends
who had been personally invited. There was a buffet breakfast, a short
welcome and introduction from their priest, and a short testimony from a
member of the congregation. He spoke about how he had often failed to
give time to his children when they needed him, about how his priorities
were often muddled, and about how he looked to gain identity from his
work but was always left feeling unsatisfied by it.

He had never done anything like this before and was eaten up with
nerves. He only spoke for a few minutes, but it was very powerful. He also
said how faith had made a difference to his life and had given him some
new priorities and a new identity, helping him to see his life in a different
way. He said he felt stupid saying all this: because men didn't usually talk
about their feelings. But he said that God was real for him. On the whole
he spent more time describing the problem than offering any great
solution. But this in itself was cathartic, and opened up some good
discussion.

At the end a story was told about identifying priorities in life. It was
about a time management consultant who in a lecture to his students
placed a glass bowl on the table and, filling it with large stones, asked
them whether there was room for anymore. 'No,' they replied, 'the bowl is
full.' 'Ah ha,' said the time management consultant and, picking up a bag
of smaller stones from under the table, placed several in around the larger
stones. 'Is it full?' he asked again. 'Probably not,' hesitated the students,
wising up to the demonstration, and a bag of sand was produced and
poured into the bowl. 'Is it full now?' they were asked. 'Yes, definitely,'
was the reply. 'No,' said the consultant and, picking up the jug that was on
the table, poured water into the bowl. 'What is the lesson of this
demonstration?' he asked. Rather depressingly the students replied that it
was amazing how much you could fit in if you really tried! 'No,' said the
consultant. 'The lesson is, get the big stones in first. If you don't, you may
never get them in at all.' In other words the key to planning, in any area of
life, is to discern what is truly important and then to give that priority in
the way we order our lives.

Those who went home from the breakfast were challenged to consider
what was truly important. The main aim of the breakfast was to think in
terms of work/home balance. But there was an obvious implication to

consider other areas of life as well. After the breakfast people were told about the nurture course that was starting in the autumn and a response card was handed round. People had a little moan about filling it in, but nearly all of them happily got on with it and it only took a few minutes.

Two people said they would like to find out more about the Christian faith. One said he would like to talk to someone. Everyone agreed they had enjoyed the event and several suggested that the church organise a breakfast like this on a regular basis.

The other outreach event was a walk for families on a Sunday with a picnic, which they hoped would emphasise the idea of faith as pilgrimage. As it turned out, it rained and everything had to happen indoors in the church hall. The walk metamorphosed into an impromptu activity day. Everyone had terrific fun. It was gathered together in a short act of worship in church. The priest spoke about the children's activities in church on Sundays and his plans for an after-school club. Four non-church families came along. Nobody signed up for the nurture course, but two years later, when the after-school club got started, two of these families became Christians and the parents went through subsequent nurture courses. The church had always identified young families as a group with whom it had really good contact. Rather than an evangelistic event, it was a more long-term ministry that turned out to be the way forward and a way of blessing this group of people and enabling them to belong to the church.

The first nurture course began with nine people: four enquirers with two sponsors acting as companions (though they weren't referred to as sponsors in the meetings), and three leaders – the priest and two apprentices. The four enquirers were a man from the breakfast, a widow contacted through a funeral visit, and a couple who had been on the fringes of church life for years and came just because they were invited.

The course ran for fifteen sessions in three blocks. At the end of each block it was possible to drop out and in the event this was exactly what the couple did at the end of the second block. But the other two went on to finish the course and at the end of the third block were welcomed into the life of the Church. Both of them had reached a point where they wanted to become Christians and join the Church. It was funny for them coming to church for the first time, but because of the fellowship they enjoyed in the group, there were people they knew who would look out for them and help them understand the liturgy. The church used a rite of welcome to show that these two fellow travellers wished to become pilgrims, to be confirmed, and to enter the life of the Church.

They were confirmed in Eastertide and the following autumn (this time pre-Advent), when the second nurture course was run, both of these new Christians invited friends of theirs to come on the course. The second course had eight enquirers, five of whom went on to be baptised or confirmed, and by this time the church was running regular evangelistic events. These in turn were providing regular opportunities for people to come and experience Christian community and begin to hear something of the Christian message, or at least a Christian perspective on some life issue. 'Regular' meant two or three times a year, though there was a move afoot to hold an annual weekend of mission, when the church would make a concerted effort to reach out to new people.

There were also now two or three people in the church who were able to lead nurture courses. They were hoping to run one in the community centre in the parish where a monthly service for the elderly had produced a number of people who had lapsed from faith and wanted a refresher course, and also a few new people wanting to explore the idea of Confirmation. The after-school club which was now running had created a whole network of contacts with young parents. There was now potential for running a small course during the day. But they were ready for this. It was possible to imagine running two or three nurture courses each year. They were adapting the material so it really fitted their parish. They were also running follow-up groups so that those who had become Christians were not left in the lurch once they had been brought to initial commitment. Something was happening in their church. Two years after beginning the nurture course, and three years after they had first begun their missionary journey, they were conscious that for the first time in twenty or thirty years the size of their congregation had grown. But even more exciting was the raising of the spiritual temperature. They were discovering for themselves that spiritual and numerical growth go hand in hand.

Their biggest surprise of all came when it was suggested they do some door-to-door visiting on a new estate in the parish. No one had ever done anything like that before and, in fact, it was the very thing they had been assured evangelism wasn't when they had begun their journey of discovery. But a small group of people decided to give it a go and knocked on doors for about an hour one evening in the early summer and asked people whether there was anything they wanted the church to pray about. To their amazement only one door was slammed in their face, and most were opened to them if not with enthusiasm then certainly not with hostility. Quite a few people requested prayers for one thing or another, and usually for loved ones who were ill or who had died. But one person was a committed Christian who had just moved into the area and was looking for a church to attend. They invited her along.

7

CONVERSION

IT IS NOT ALWAYS POSSIBLE to identify the moment along the way when a fellow traveller becomes a pilgrim. Some people do have dramatic conversion experiences and are completely turned around; others encounter a series of signposts which steadily change their direction; others find that it is only in looking back that they can see the new route that has been taken. Whatever the individual experience, the term 'pilgrim' describes well the new orientation of life.

All of us experience life as a journey, but a life without God, however rich and meaningful, is going nowhere. Death is the final destination and then nothing. Faith changes life in all sorts of ways, but most dramatically the journey of life now becomes a journey home. We find the centre of our life is no longer located within ourselves, or in what we see around us, but in God. We let go of the things of this world and cleave to the things of heaven. But far from losing our joy in the world around us, in our relationships and our passions, it is given back to us tenfold. By putting Christ at the centre of our lives we discover the radical gospel truth that he has put us at the centre of his. To be a pilgrim, then, is to be in right relationship with God and in right relationship with the world. Our life has a destination and a purpose, but, because we also know God as the source of all life, we are given an abundance of joy in the journey. This is focused in the incarnation – God's total identification with all that is created – and in the ascension – God's taking of creation into the Godhead itself. To know that you are a pilgrim is the first stage of Christian discipleship. It gives a new direction to life. From this point on we don't talk about the journey *to* faith, but the journey *of* faith.

REPENTANCE
To speak of a new direction implies there was an old one. Although we live in a society which has largely stopped believing in sin, pilgrims will still be aware that life is changing. The more they glimpse the new direction of life that the Christian faith offers, the more they will be aware of the failures and shortcomings of what went before. Life will no longer be lived for self alone; it will be focused on God.

Bernard of Clairvaux spoke of the four stages of love that make up the Christian pilgrimage:

1. love of self for self's sake
2. love of God for self's sake
3. love of God for God's sake
4. love of self for God's sake.

The true aim of the Christian journey is to arrive at a point of complete love of self and love of God, but for God's sake: for God's praise and glory, not our own. On the way there is the narrowly selfish love of God for what we can get out of it, and also the hideously religious love of God and life-denying abandonment of everything else (and there is an awful lot of this around in the church!). As we walk the way of faith, so we learn these lessons of love. But the old way, which we leave behind, is startlingly captured in the phrase 'Love of self for self's sake', for it is the beginning of all sin. It is the denial of our interdependence with one another and with the creation; it is the denial that we are children of God, and made for relationship with God. It is that fatal and bruising tendency to put self first and imagine ourselves as the centre of the universe.

Some Christians say that we should tell people the bad news first. That before we tell them the good news of salvation in Christ we should tell them the bad news about the reality of sin and the damage it does. I do not take this view, and I do not think it is the catholic way. As we discussed in the opening chapter, our motivation for evangelism can't just be saving lost souls from hell. We must leave issues of final judgement to God alone. Our task is to share the good news of the fullness of life that we have found in Christ. We remind people that they belong to one another and that they belong to God. Many people in our society today suffer enough from low self-esteem and lack of self-worth without receiving a further battering from the Church. But neither should we duck the issue of sin. After all, the gospel is about forgiveness.

As people begin to discover the reality of Christian faith on the journey of nurture, so there will come a point where it is natural and appropriate to speak of repentance. The literal meaning of 'to repent' is 'to turn around'. It is the conscious reorientation of life: it is when someone begins to see their life as a pilgrimage, and not just a journey. Michael Marshall puts it well when he says that repentance is not seeing a different world 'so much as the same world differently'.[1]

As people proceed on a nurture course and discover faith dawning within them, or for that matter if faith comes suddenly, the final stages of preparation for initiation need to include a definite invitation to take seriously the gospel call to repentance.

COMMITMENT

Becoming a Christian is a response of our whole being to the love of God. Decisively, it is a response of the will: we decide to follow Christ and to try to live our lives by all that that entails. Faith may dawn slowly, but a decision to become a Christian must have its reality in an actual turning-point. The journey always reaches a point where there is a decision: shall I go on? Can I take all that the Christian path holds? If the actual point of decision does not happen in the dramatic circumstances of a conversion experience (and it probably won't for most people), then baptism or Confirmation provides an opportunity.

The liturgy can do a really good job of bringing people face to face with the new direction their lives are taking. The rites of baptism and Confirmation, or affirmation of baptismal faith, clearly contain prayers of repentance and reorientation. Indeed, the language of *Common Worship* is stark and uncompromising:

> In baptism God calls us out of darkness into his marvellous light.
> To follow Christ means dying to sin and rising to new life with him.
> Therefore I ask:
>
> Do you reject the devil and all rebellion against God?
> Do you renounce the deceit and corruption of evil?
> Do you repent of the sins that separate us from God and
>   neighbour?
> Do you turn to Christ as Saviour?
> Do you submit to Christ as Lord?
> Do you come to Christ, the way, the truth and the life?[2]

However, many new Christians will have particular issues that they will want to deal with in private. This can be done through prayer and through counselling, especially a ministry of listening. Most new Christians will also find it very helpful to make some sort of sacramental confession.

The sacrament of reconciliation is particularly helpful for people who are at this stage in their journey since it helps them to appropriate the full impact of the gospel. Reconciliation *is* the gospel. Christ makes union with God possible and available. And all of Christ's ministry is itself the decisive reaching out of the apostolic God. God comes to look for us. It is this emphasis that Henri Nouwen draws out as he reflects upon Jesus' story of the Prodigal Son: a story that has so influenced our understanding of God's merciful love.

> For most of my life I have struggled to find God, to know God, to love God. I have tried hard to follow the guidelines of the spiritual life and to avoid the many temptations to dissipate myself. I have

failed many times but always tried again, even when I was close to despair. Now I wonder whether I have sufficiently realised that during all this time God has been trying to find me, to know me, and to love me. The question is not 'How am I to find God?' but 'How am I to let myself be found by him?' The question is not 'How am I to know God?' but 'How am I to let myself be known by God?' And, finally, the question is not 'How am I to love God?' but 'How am I to let myself be loved by God?' God is looking into the distance for me, trying to find me and longing to bring me home. It might sound strange, but God wants to find me as much as, if not more than, I want to find God. God is not the patriarch who stays at home, doesn't move, and expects his children to come to him, apologise for their aberrant behaviour, beg for forgiveness, and promise to do better. To the contrary he leaves the house, ignoring his dignity by running towards them, pays no heed to apologies and promises of change, and brings them to the table richly prepared for them.

I am beginning to see how radically the character of my spiritual journey will change when I no longer think of God as hiding out and making it as difficult as possible for me to find him, but, instead, as the one who is looking for me while I am hiding. When I look through God's eyes at my lost self and discover God's joy at my coming home, then my life may become less anguished and more trusting. Wouldn't it be good to increase God's joy by letting God find me and carry me home?[3]

The cross is the ultimate meeting point between humanity and God. It is where we see how far God travels to reach us. It is a place of ignominy – the scandalous death of an innocent man reveals our capacity for inhumanity. It is a place of triumph – the self-giving love of Jesus reveals the loving heart of God. Baptism is our sharing in this triumph: it reveals the new direction of life as well as wiping away the harmful effects of the old one. The sacrament of reconciliation is a personal way of receiving and re-appropriating this gospel truth. It provides a way of making a personal step of faith to mirror the public step of initiation.[4] Through it we acknowledge our need; we make ourselves vulnerable to God. We allow ourselves to be found and healed. It is powerful good news for people to hear the words of absolution being spoken to them personally, and to be set free from the sin which had stifled their spirit and which they had so often sought to suppress (this is what we do with sin in an age which pretends everything is relative).

We need to understand not just the abundant grace of the sacrament, but the psychological significance of being able to make a definite and personal step forward. As well as encouraging people to share in the sacrament of reconciliation, it is important to spend time with them individually and to help them make a prayer of personal commitment, if they have not already done so.

Giving people the opportunity to make a response is of prime importance to the evangelistic process; it is vital in establishing people in the faith. This is an important part of the role of a nurture group leader – one which is sadly all-too-easily ducked. If courses are being led by lay people, clergy may want to become involved at this crucial stage. Many clergy have had little experience of seeing adults come to faith, but we must not shy away from encouraging a definite response.

The value of the personal encounter and response provided by the sacrament of reconciliation is also something Christians of other traditions will want to take seriously. In recent years many Christians are rediscovering the power and efficacy of this sacrament to enable people to lay down the burdens of the past and set the compass of their life towards the new humanity given us by Christ.

I am also mindful of how few opportunities there are in most Anglican churches for people to make any sort of personal response to Christ. There needs to be more teaching about the availability of the sacrament of reconciliation and its converting power. Many charismatic parishes are very good at offering what they call a 'time of ministry' at the end of a service. Churches of a more liturgical tradition could also provide regular opportunities for people to make their confession, receive prayer for healing, or just have someone to talk to about where they are on their journey. These times for response with prayer and blessing could be built into the liturgical life of the church.

When I was a Diocesan Missioner there were a number of occasions when, having spoken about the importance of response as part of an ordinary Sunday preaching engagement, instead of standing at the door to shake hands at the end of the service, I told the congregation I would be sitting in the Lady Chapel in case anyone wanted to talk or pray about their own response to God. On every single occasion people came.

THE STEP OF FAITH

This stage in the nurture process requires a great deal of care. On the one hand, we need to be prepared to go the second mile, conscious that people's development in faith rarely matches the timetables of our nurture courses and, on the other, we need to be ready to challenge for a response, helping people to make the decision that is clearly emerging into view. Sometimes we just need to have the courage to ask people what is preventing them from taking the next step. The best midwives know when the expectant mother needs to push and does not shy away from giving a command.

But often people's reticence is as much about apologetics as it is about evangelism. Quite often people are prevented from making the step of faith because there are barriers in the way. We need to be ready and able to deal with their issues, even if it will frequently be the case that we have no conclusive answers. Being prepared to listen will always prove helpful. We need to remember that Jesus was called Emmanuel – the God with us in the midst of difficulty and suffering – as well as Jesus, the God who saves.

We need to care tenderly for those who are coming to faith. We also need to challenge boldly for a response. The Holy Spirit evangelises, but if we faithfully attend to this ministry, acting as living signposts and good companions, we will see people make the step of faith, and there are few things more joyful and fulfilling in Christian ministry.

Conversion can be summed up in a phrase I have used several times in this book, but not yet unpacked: the free response of love. I find it a very helpful phrase. First, it is a description of what God has done in Christ: his searching and caring for us. Second, it is a description of an awakening within us. We find ourselves to be the beloved of God and we offer our lives to him.

Paul uses the imagery of marriage and adoption to describe this transaction of love. It is like being adopted into a family and yet being regarded as a first-born son or daughter (see Galatians 4:5-7). It is also like being married. Jesus' words on the cross, 'It is finished' (John 19:30), carry the same meaning as the promise the bridegroom makes in the marriage service when he says, 'I will.' God, in Christ, pledges his troth to us, for richer for poorer, in sickness and in health, for this time and for-ever. The words of the marriage liturgy are: 'All that I am I give to you and all that I have I share with you'.[5] This is the given of faith; this is what God has done for us regardless of whether we respond at all. But when we see what he has done, when we experience it for ourselves – however dimly – we know ourselves in Henri Nouwen's words 'being found'. And at this moment the drama of salvation, just like the drama of the wedding service, turns to the other partner. We are asked whether we will take Jesus 'to have and to hold, to love and to cherish, for this time and forever'. When we say 'Yes' to God – in the same way that Mary said 'Yes' to the angel, the disciples said 'Yes' when they dropped everything to follow Jesus, and so many millions of Christian people have done down the centuries – we make a free response of love. It is the Spirit speaking within us, but it is also the voice of our true self, finding that the love of God is the source of a love we have always longed for.

And because it is love it has to be free, for love never insists on its own way (cf. 1 Corinthians 13:5). Take away a little of the freedom and you take away all of the love. That is why on the Emmaus Road Jesus was not recognised. What God longs for is love, and nothing less than love will do. Edward Pusey described the mystery of God's relationship with human beings in these words:

> We know not why our free will is so precious in the eyes of God that he waits for us, pleads with us, draws us, allures us, wins us, over-powers us with his love; but he will not force us. He made us to be like him. And what is this but to be holy?[6]

It is this loving holiness that God longs for. It freely flows from the abundance of God's heart, and it can flow back from human hearts. It is for this reason that God waits till we allow ourselves to be found. Then Jesus' arms stretched out on the cross are not just a sign of all we do to crucify love: they are there to embrace us and take us home.

We may reject God's offer. But even our rejection cannot stop him loving us.

Example

The two people who came to faith on the first nurture course at St Mary's were confirmed on the Second Sunday of Easter. One of them was also baptised. Their sponsors and a large group from the congregation accompanied them to the church on the other side of the diocese where the service took place. It was very moving.

On the day before the Confirmation both individuals had made their confession, but in the case of the person who was being baptised the declaration of absolution was delayed so that the baptism itself – entry into the sacramental life as well as the beginning of the Christian life – could be the moment of forgiveness. Neither of them particularly wanted to make a confession but when it was explained that it was a chance to make a personal response to God in preparation for the public response of the Confirmation, they welcomed the opportunity. It was like a spring-clean, making room for God and making space for his Spirit to dwell within them. By this time neither of them needed convincing of the reality of sin: the more they learned about Jesus the more they realised that their biggest failings were not what they had done, but what they had failed to do. It was a big step actually to share their failings with someone else. But after they had made their confession they were filled with a great joy. Not only had it been good to let go of some of the baggage from the past, it was a wonderful feeling to know that they were loved and accepted.

A few days after the Confirmation a work colleague of one of those who had been confirmed, commenting on her new-found faith, said that the Church was full of hypocrites. 'Yes,' she replied, 'and there is always room for one more!' The truth that the church is a band of pilgrims, repentant sinners taking the cure, was really beginning to take hold in their lives and in the life of the whole church. The moment of confirmation by the bishop seemed like a turning-point – a real affirmation of all that had already happened, and a new beginning for life. The knowledge that they were children of God which had been awakened within them was now matched by a bold determination to live as citizens of heaven.

8

HELPING PEOPLE TO GROW IN THEIR FAITH/BUILDING COMMUNITY

COMMITMENT TO JESUS and membership of the Church is not the end of the story, but just the beginning. The journey *to* faith becomes the journey *of* faith. As Bishop Michael Marshall has noted, the aim of evangelism is not to drag the world into the church, but to pour a Spirit-filled church into the world. Our aim is not more church members, but active disciples. We therefore need to do a thorough job of initiation, and this always requires more than a course of enquiry, however effective it might be. What people explored as they were nurtured in the way of faith needs to be built upon so that those who have come to know their life as a pilgrimage are also conscious of the apostolic call: like the first disciples they too are being commissioned to live and share the gospel, beckoning others to walk the way of Christ.

But there is another paradox in the Christian life that we need to explore. The people Jesus called to follow him – his disciples – are the same people he sent out as his ambassadors – his apostles. We are called to be both. Or as I put it in the first part of the book: our vocation is to be the gathered-in *and* the sent-out church. The conjugate foci of growing faith are the call to be both disciple and apostle; to be following Christ and to be sent out by Christ.

This double vocation was beautifully represented for me when I recently visited the reconstructed anchorite cell of Mother Julian of Norwich. There she lived with a window on the church, enabling her to participate in worship and receive the sacraments, and a window on the world where she could minister to others. This is the way Christian people are called to live their lives, and it is not a matter of serving one's apprenticeship as a disciple and then graduating to become an apostle. Every day I need to live as a disciple of Christ, conscious of my own need of God's grace and forgiveness. And every day I need to live as an apostle, conscious of my own responsibility to live a Christlike life and communicate the values and the beauty of the gospel to those around me. In this respect every Christian is called to be a witness to Christ. We rightly discern that some people have a particular calling to serve as an evangelist, one who is gifted to communicate the gospel and enable others to discover faith. We have also noted that evangelism is a ministry that belongs to the whole church and we all have different parts to play. But all of us – because of our baptism into Christ's dying and rising – are called to be witnesses.

In this we have no choice. It is no use saying that being a witness is not our calling. Once people have discovered that we go to church, whether we like it or not they will be evaluating the church and the gospel on the evidence of our lives. And if our lives are indistinguishable from every-body else's, then no wonder our evangelism is ineffective. This does not mean we are supposed to be better than everybody else. It is the great English heresy to believe that being a Christian equals being good. What really marks out a Christian life is not so much our goodness, but the generosity, tolerance, kindness and clemency that flow from our knowing how much we need God ourselves. It is our need of God, and his loving mercy to us, that enables us to be more merciful, more humble, more generous and more forgiving with those around us. In this way, more than any other, we witness to Christ.

It is also in this way that the most fruitful and effective evangelism takes place. For the best evangelism of all is the Christlike witness of ordinary Christian people in their ordinary daily lives. This is the evan-gelism I long for and it happens when the church is so rooted in Christ that our lives become translucent of the gospel. Everything else that I am say-ing about evangelism is secondary to this truth and contingent upon it. Unless we are taking seriously the call to live a holy life, then everything else we do is bound to flounder.

THE APOSTOLIC LIFE
In order to help people grow in their faith and discover their share in the apostolic vocation, the following aspects of Christian discipleship need to be explored:

• prayer
• fellowship
• lifestyle
• service
• witness
• knowledge of the faith.

It would take another book to cover these aspects adequately, but because it is so important to stress that evangelism is about making disciples I need to comment on each of them briefly. Furthermore, I want to draw attention to the context in which these attributes can be learnt and developed. From this point on whenever the word 'growth' or 'disciple' is used, I am referring to this twin vocation of disciple *and* apostle, whereby we grow in relationship with God, within the household of the church and in service to the world. This is the big vision of evangelism, Christ's own commission to his church that we make disciples.

Prayer

To grow in the Christian life means to grow in relationship with God. Such growth happens through a life of prayer and through finding a way of prayer that suits our personality and our circumstances. Gerard Hughes has said that the main job of bishops and clergy in this new millennium is to teach people to pray. We have already discussed the nature of prayer as our response to the love of God we find in Christ. But how does this work out in a disciplined life of prayer?

Have you ever had the experience of driving on the motorway, noticing the petrol gauge is about to tick onto the red, when a sign comes up telling you there are services in five miles and in fifty miles? You look again at the petrol gauge and decide that you can make it to the services that are fifty miles away and drive past the petrol station. Of course, no extra time is saved by doing so. The process of filling up with petrol requires the same amount of time whether it is done at the first petrol station or the second. Indeed, by waiting, a great deal of time may be wasted! But although I have never yet run out of petrol on the motorway I have often got very close, driving on empty and nearly running dry.

The first thing to say about prayer is that we need regular times of prayer – though it can take many different forms. Many people are running on empty. They simply don't pray. Driving past the filling stations they imagine the Christian life can be self-sustained.

Helping people to establish a simple rule of life where times and patterns of prayer are woven into daily life is an invaluable way of helping them connect with the resources of the Christian tradition and with the goodness and energy of God.[1]

But prayer is much more than filling up. We need regular times of prayer, but most of all we need to be prayerful. St Paul says, 'Rejoice always, pray without ceasing' (1 Thessalonians 5:16–17). I don't think he means that we should do that activity we call prayer without ceasing. He means that we should make our life a prayer. We should seek to make every moment of our lives an offering of praise to God. We should allow every moment of our lives to be shaped by God. Just as the car is made to be driven and not meant to be kept in the garage, so our life is to be lived. 'I came', says Jesus, 'that they may have life, and have it abundantly' (John 10:10). Fullness of life can only be enjoyed when we live our lives in community with God. This is the heart of the Christian revelation.

Jesus is the one through whom we can have community with God and by whom we can be taught how to live fully human lives. Hence my working definition of prayer is: 'The lover coming into the presence of the Beloved and saying "I love you".'

To help people grow in this loving relationship with God there needs to be regular teaching about prayer: weeks of guided prayer, retreats, pilgrimages and schools of prayer. Literature needs to be made available and those with a calling for spiritual direction need to be encouraged and authorised to exercise this ministry in the local church. So much of all we hope to achieve in the Christian life rests on the spiritual reawakening the life of prayer evokes and is hampered and compromised by the low priority it usually takes.

Fellowship

To grow in the Christian life means to grow in relationship with one another. You can't be a Christian on your own. Paul's astonishing theology of the church describes us as the body of Christ, intimately related to God through Christ and intimately related to each other. Therefore, growing in community with each other can never be an optional extra for the Christian. We need to take seriously one another's needs and appreciate and develop one another's gifts: caring for one another is at the heart of what it means to be a disciple. As we have already noted in connection with the fourfold vocation of the church to be one, holy, catholic and apostolic, unity is at the heart of the church's vocation and the very word 'catholic' points towards the wholeness God wills for us. If we are to help people grow in relationship with each other, we need to give attention to the social and communal side of church life.

Lifestyle and service

To grow in the Christian life also means that our own lives will begin to mirror the life of Christ. Of course, none of us can ever achieve the standard his life set, but we pursue the way of holiness both through our prayer and through the life we lead, seeking to ensure that our standards and values reflect the values and standards of the gospel.

The question posed earlier in relation to the ministry of the church is also relevant for our own lives: is my life a blessing to those around me? To what extent do people meet Christ when they meet me? These are hard questions, but facing up to them is vital if we are to allow the faith we celebrate on Sunday to shape the lives we lead Monday to Saturday.

Our Christian standards and values should affect the whole of our lives: our decision making; our use of time; the priorities we have; the way we fill in our tax return; the political judgements we make; the attitudes we have to those around us; and so on.

The catholic tradition in the Church of England has always had a determined concern for social justice. In many churches this vision is blurred by preoccupation with other concerns, or simply lost through the fatigue that is brought on by decline. But when we think of the great names of priests who pioneered the second wave of the Anglo-Catholic revival in the Church of England – men like Dolling, Stanton, Wainwright, Louder and Jellicoe – they stand out not just because of their powerful personal holiness, but because faith for them overflowed into action. Their churches grew and had influence and impact because of the beauty of the worship, but also because of the practical concern for justice and a bias for the poor and underprivileged. Catholic parishes and all Christian men and women need again to be in the forefront of campaigning to end poverty, to address the global imbalance between north and south, to defend human rights, and to safeguard the bio-diversity of the planet. All of these issues are of concern to God and are part of God's mission and purpose. If the work of evangelism is to make disciples who participate in the mission of God, then the fruits of this ministry will be seen not only in more people coming to faith and churches growing, but in the building of a society whose values and standards are shaped by God. And, of course, as people see the church speak out against injustice and stand up for the poor, they will be attracted to the church. 'Love people until they ask why'[2] was how I heard it put recently.

The question we asked earlier, 'How can we serve the people with whom we have contact?' can also be expressed, 'How can we serve the community of which we are a part?' Ultimately our evangelism is not just to individuals but to the whole of human society.

Witness and knowledge of the faith

As Christians we need to grow in our awareness that, whether we like it or not, our lives are an advertisement for the gospel. What sort of a witness are they? The Scriptures teach us that we should all be able to give a reason for the hope that is within us (1 Peter 3:15). This oft-quoted text is preceded by the observation that in our hearts Christ should be sanctified as Lord, again making the connection between what we receive and experience in our hearts and what we share with others. To grow in the Christian life, therefore, means to grow in our knowledge of God and in the faith we share.

As I said earlier in the book, every Christian should be able to tell two beautiful and unique stories:

• the story of what God has done in his or her own life
• the story of what God has done in Christ.

We simply cannot live the apostolic life unless we are able to speak about our faith both as personal testimony – what it has meant for our life – and as saving truth – what it means for every human life and for the whole of creation.

We have already spoken about all Christian people being called to be witnesses and having a share in God's ministry of evangelism. Some will also have a particular calling to be an evangelist, with a gift for explaining and commending faith and enabling people to find Christ. We need to recognise and affirm this vocation. We need more catholic evangelists. We also need to develop a ministry of evangelism in every catholic parish and share the insights of a catholic approach to evangelism with all Christians.

But we also need a theologically literate church. While we are quite good at equipping one or two of the keener members of the congregation to go and undertake some sort of theological study, the vast majority of our people have only a very slender grasp on the intellectual credibility of the Christian faith. Yet we live in a culture where many people, who themselves have hardly any knowledge of the Christian faith, blithely assume that science has disproved Christianity and that the human sciences have rendered it irrelevant. We have allowed the truth about God as revealed in Jesus Christ to become a private option in the eat-as-much-as-you-like buffet of post-modern beliefs. Very few Christians have the confidence to speak about their faith as public truth, nor the lived experience of God to speak about faith as ontological reality. The two go together. The proclamation of Christian faith needs to be credible and incredible: sanely argued so that its historic roots and intellectual coherence can be presented, and wonderfully celebrated because it takes us beyond ourselves, breaking down the carefully constructed walls around our comfort zones and changing lives.

To put it bluntly, we have not been good at teaching people the faith. This is a massive task, and it is an area of massive failure. One of the keys to becoming an evangelising church is this equipping of the people of God to be able to speak about their faith personally and convincingly. The local church is the place where people should be learning about their faith and exploring its relevance for life. By this I don't mean learning glib answers to fend off the serious questions that our culture asks of faith, but a real engagement with the big questions of meaning and purpose that shape every human life and demand attention. The Christian faith can never be reduced to a set of answers or propositions, but it can be a well of experience and theological reflection from which we can draw insights that can shape debate. It is only when Christian people are thinking theologically and living in community with God that faith can again shape the decisions of our nation. When the whole church grows in the knowledge of its faith, our witness and evangelism will extend to the whole culture and to the whole of society and not just those individuals we meet in the networks of our lives. This is part of the big vision we need to hang on to.

HOW AND WHERE CAN WE DEVELOP A MINISTRY OF DISCIPLESHIP?

Most people will have no difficulty in agreeing with the above, though they may wish to add to the menu of what is offered to help people grow in their faith. The question is one of context – not what we do, but where and how we do it. Most of the models for discipleship come from evangelical churches and don't translate well into churches whose corporate life is shaped by a liturgical and sacramental tradition. However, a certain humility is recommended in recognising that there are many things we can learn from the way other churches have tackled this. But we need to find a way that sits with our own ethos and spirituality. We may also need to let go of some things. The growth we long to see will not come through the unchanged diet of worship alone. Of course, the Eucharist itself will remain at the centre of our life, the place more than any other where we are fed and nourished on our Christian journey. But preaching alone cannot enable people to understand faith, and there are other issues that urgently need to be explored and that require a context that church on Sunday morning rarely provides. There needs to be a 'somewhere else' where issues of growth can be explored.

Here are some ideas of how this ministry can be taken forward.

1. Develop the potential of what you already do

Every meeting has the potential to be a place where issues of discipleship are looked at. Instead of thinking about what other meetings you can put on, look at the meetings you already have and see what else can be built into them. There is no reason why half an hour at every PCC meeting cannot be spent looking at the Scriptures or exploring some aspect of discipleship. You might actually find it transforms the way you deal with the rest of the business. Also there is no unwritten rule stating that church meetings always have to imitate the way the world works: our agendas do not always need to be driven by the immediate or the urgent or even the strategic. We could spend more time praying together in our meetings and waiting on God. Many catholic parishes always begin their meeting with a Eucharist and this practice already points the way forward. By celebrating the Eucharist together we declare that our primary reason for meeting – whatever else is on the agenda and however urgent it appears – is to worship God. Why not develop this a little and include other aspects of discipleship within the meeting? And this could apply to every meeting of every group, from the parent and toddlers' group to the finance subcommittee. Make praying together and reflecting on the common vocation to live a Christian life the main item on every agenda.

2. Develop the church's corporate life through cells

Influenced by some rapidly growing Asian churches, transitioning to a cellular model of church life has become one of the latest evangelical bandwagons to roll into town. However, like most new ideas it is very old indeed. It reminds us of a basic insight that the Christian life is life lived in community and that we should give expression to our corporateness in smaller and more intimate gatherings than can usually be accommodated on a Sunday. Building on the success and effectiveness of home groups, cells go a couple of steps further in identifying the cell – the small group – as the primary unit of the church. Whereas home groups were effectively small groups that met 'after church', cells are church. They are the place where people meet, worship and witness. A wealth of literature is available about cell church and how it can work, though my experience is that in many cases churches in Britain have simply re-branded their home groups as cells and really the model is not very different. However, there are some churches who have completely re-worked how they operate so that the cell is the centre of church life.

There is clearly a link here with some of the Roman Catholic base ecclesial communities and, indeed, unless there is a rise in Roman Catholic vocations to the priesthood, it will be interesting to see if such a model of church becomes more widespread. For Anglican catholic parishes, although it is hard to imagine the cell replacing the Eucharist as the centre of the church's life, there is a need to gather people together in smaller groups and the biblical image of the different cells making up the body is clearly an attractive one.

In the 1970s there was a catholic parish in Lewisham[3] that split its congregation into what I think were called mini-parishes. In these smaller, geographically based groupings the Eucharist was celebrated in people's homes, the Scriptures were broken open, fellowship was enjoyed and the faith was explored. It came to be expected that membership of the church meant more than attendance at Sunday worship. You were also part of a mini-parish, whether you liked it or not, or whether you attended or not. Whether that group was expected to evangelise I don't know, but clearly it has that potential.

Developing such a model and keeping it Eucharistic obviously requires priests, and there are less around than in the 1970s. However, it does not require the Eucharist to be celebrated at every meeting and can therefore be lay led. What such a group provides is a context of worship and community where other theological issues can be explored and where service and witness can take place. Such groups will therefore be more than study groups. They deliberately seek to recreate that model of church glimpsed in Acts 2:42 where we read: 'They devoted themselves to the apostles' teaching and fellowship, to the breaking of bread and the prayers.' It was this simple and attractive living out of the Christian faith in community that was so magnetic to others. We need to strive to find a way of giving this expression in our own culture. We also need to recognise that it may not necessarily be in each other's homes that these cells are born. It could be in the workplace, or, as we shall see in a moment, in fresh ways of expressing our corporate life.

3. Try 'long church' – a different approach to celebrating the Eucharist

On my visits to North America I have been enormously impressed by the different attitude to Sunday morning that most Christians have. As well as a commitment to worship there is also a commitment to some sort of learning or faith-developing activity. This is often called 'Adult Sunday School', which does not strike me as a terribly attractive title, but what they do there is extremely attractive. At many Episcopalian churches either before or after worship there will be breakfast and then a programme of learning that people sign up for.

Let us compare this to the English situation. I well remember my first Sunday as an incumbent. As with most churches there was an unwritten contract stating that worship lasted an hour, after which coffee was available for the very keen, and the whole thing would be over in an hour and a half. Then people were free to go. And woe betide any priest who broke this contract. Five or ten minutes' leeway was permitted, but after that you were in deep trouble!

This scenario is replicated in many churches up and down the country. To complicate the situation further we then devote five of these precious sixty minutes to notices, where we try to persuade people to return to church on Tuesday evening for the PCC, or Wednesday evening for the home group, or Thursday morning for the Bible study, and so on.

My first suggestion is that we re-negotiate the contract. Why not once a month – or even once a quarter – celebrate the Eucharist differently? Even extending the celebration by half an hour would create the possibility of a space where some growth activity could take place. An hour, and you have the possibility of building some cellular structure into the regular worshipping life of the church. This could either be done within the worship itself, celebrating the liturgy of the Word in a new way, or it could be done as an optional extra, but as part of the Sunday morning provision. A church in Cumnor near Oxford has something like an adult Sunday school on a monthly basis. From 9.00 a.m. breakfast is served in the church hall; from 9.30 to 10.45 a discussion takes place involving

teenagers as well as adults linking in with the thematic teaching programme of the church and therefore flowing into the service which starts
at 11.00. It is entirely lay-led.

At St Thomas', Huddersfield, a church made famous by liturgical
innovations and re-ordering while Fr Richard Giles was vicar, a monthly
meeting was developed as its way of dealing with the question of growth.
I served in this church for eight years and was asked to help them think
through the issues of ongoing growth. Home groups and cells had never
really become established and almost in desperation at one church
meeting we found ourselves asking what did work for us when it came to
faith development. The answer was 'not much'. What did go well was the
Mass on Sunday morning and midweek festivals when people also turned
out in good numbers. This was a church with a rich and stimulating liturgical life. It became clear that the context for helping people grow in faith
would also need to be liturgical. What emerged was a monthly gathering
of the church within the context of an extended Eucharist. The joke was,
'You've heard of high church and low church, now try long church!'

People gathered at about 6.30 and the Eucharist began quite informally,
but with the normal greeting and penitential rite. Next, for the liturgy of
the Word there would be teaching and group work dealing with a particular aspect of faith development, along the lines we discussed earlier. This
would take about an hour. Then supper was shared, with people taking it
in turns to provide food for everyone else. After supper the community
gathered together more formally around the altar to exchange the peace,
pray the Eucharistic Prayer and receive Communion. At about 9.00 p.m.
the Eucharist finished. Whereas home groups in the parish had only ever
attracted a small proportion of the regular worshipping community, this
model attracted well over half. It is a model that I think could be used by
many catholic parishes as a way of tackling the vital issue of faith
development within the context of the Eucharist. As time passed, it was
also found that this celebration of the Eucharist, although much longer
than on Sunday morning, was actually the best one to introduce new
people to. Its more interactive and exploratory approach enabled people to
feel included more quickly.

PASTORAL CARE

Finally in this chapter, we need to look at the issue of pastoral care. For
many churches the problem is not so much getting people as keeping
them. If all the people who had joined the church over the last twenty years
had stayed, our situation today would be remarkably transformed. There
are many reasons why people lapse. One, as we have seen, is the failure to
take the ongoing process of initiation seriously, especially in the first

couple of years of a new Christian's life. Enabling people to grow in faith in the ways described above will begin to make a difference, the cumulative impact of which will be seen after a few years. Even if only a small proportion of people join in with these growth activities, it is still important to persevere. Any strategy for growth must have at its heart the building up in faith of the people of God, even if this only means a small group of people at the heart of the church. We would be wise to remember the disproportionate amount of time Jesus gave to a few people.

But another issue that hampers growth and causes people to lapse is a lack of pastoral care. Rather than seeing pastoral care as somehow separate from evangelism, we could argue we have not been pastoral enough, both when it comes to those inside the church and those outside it. As we have already seen, it is in offering real care and service that the best strategy for evangelism can be developed. Being cared for is also central to the life of a Christian community. Once again it brings us back to the importance of our belonging to each other within a church which is catholic as well as apostolic.

As a church grows in size it becomes much harder to maintain a system of pastoral care where the priest feels able to know and regularly visit every member of the congregation. This model of pastoral care creates a growth ceiling of around 100 to 150 people. Many catholic parishes, often subconsciously, operate this pastoral model. The church is a loving, caring hospitable community – like a family where everyone knows everyone else and is also known by the priest – who, significantly, is called 'Father' or 'Mother'.

I remember my own experience of being priest in charge of a growing congregation. It seemed to me that as the congregation grew the only option was for me to work harder in order to maintain the creative environment that was attracting people in the first place. However, as the church grew, it was my model of leadership that was becoming the problem. I had to find a new way of pastoring the church that moved from my being the one who provided the pastoral care to my being the one who ensured pastoral care was provided. I still wanted a church that was welcoming and caring, but that welcome and that care had to be expressed by the congregation and not by me alone. It is easy to say this, but it is very hard for many priests of a catholic tradition to make this transition. So much of our identity as priests is tied up with this model of ministry. Hence, the fact that we like to be called 'Father' or 'Mother'. Whereas a priest of a catholic parish thinks not knowing someone's name in the congregation is a sign of failure, a priest of an evangelical parish sees it as a sign of success.

A growing church needs a new model for pastoral care. This could be through regular groups – cells, for example – which provide a place where people can feel known and cared for, but, as we have already noted, such groups don't always work well in catholic parishes (though this is not a reason not to try). Alternatively, it could be through developing a lay-led pastoral care team so that the work of pastoral care is shared by the church. Whichever option is chosen it is vital for some form of pastoral care to be established so that the church does not find that as fast as their evangelism brings people into the church through the front door, their lack of pastoral care allows them to slip out through the back door. The basic principle is that pastoral care has to become *one another* care.[4]

It is also important to say that, whichever option is chosen, the lay leaders of these groups are crucial and the priest must spend a lot of time in their ongoing support.

The first sign that these changes are necessary is usually that the clergy are working too hard trying to keep the show on the road and are in danger of burning themselves out. However, the implications are wider than just pastoral care. The realisation that there needs to be some shared pastoral care leads quickly to the realisation that there needs to be shared leadership in the church. When a church does start to grow it isn't just because it has developed proper structures for evangelism, nurture and growth, central though these three ministries are: it will be because most things about the church are healthy and attractive, not least the worship on Sunday morning. But it is a sad fact of church growth that as the number of people coming to church increases, the quality of church life often decreases. Sharing leadership and developing and using the gifts of others can be effective ways of addressing this problem.

APOSTOLIC SPIRITUALITY

Returning to where we began, we need an apostolic spirituality for an apostolic life: an 'as you go' spirituality.

Robert Warren defines spirituality as 'how we encounter God and how that encounter is sustained'.[5] At the heart of a renewed catholic spirituality will be the Eucharist. Here God is encountered in his Word, in the sacrament and in the people who bear his name. Eucharistic theology enshrines the gospel paradox that things need to be broken open before they can be shared. It is with broken bread that we share the body of Christ.

But we also need to be a people who regularly break open the Word of God. This needs to happen in our liturgy, in our groups and in our homes. The Scriptures need a greater place of honour in catholic spirituality.

And we need to be a people who are ourselves broken open in love to one another and in service to the world. It is these acts of sacrificial love that will, more than anything, begin to convey the radical truth of the gospel. It is in service to one another that we shall sustain our encounter with Jesus.

We need to be a people who drink deeply from the sacramental well. The sacraments are given to the Church as channels of grace. There needs to be more teaching in our churches about the evangelical power of the sacraments, especially the Eucharist, reconciliation and healing. The world cries out for value and meaning, for forgiveness and for healing. These are the very things entrusted to us in the sacramental life. We can receive from Jesus the new value of being citizens of heaven; we can feed at his table; we can hear his words of absolution; we can be assured of the ultimate promise that all will be well; and in the midst of terrible suffering we can discover his passion and death, and come to understand that the God who made the world, not only loves it, but has entered it. He is the God who seeks out every human heart and who comes to listen, to serve and to love.

In these ways we will, in our own day, carry the marks of the apostolic Church which we identified in the first chapter – a lively and credible faith, resonating with the culture of the day and testified by holy lives.

In the final chapter we will look at how we can evangelise through worship, examining how we can let the gospel shape our worship and discovering what fresh expressions of church need to arise out of our evangelistic ministry.

ONGOING GROWTH
A missionary church needs structures to maintain the growth of new Christians and preserve the intimacy and fellowship of a growing congregation. The chief elements in these structures are:

1. ongoing groups for growth
2. shared pastoral care
3. shared leadership.

Their establishment will be particularly hard on the priest who will have to move from being the person who provides the primary care for the church to being the one who ensures primary care is provided. This is a new role, but no less priestly. The priest needs to become the servant of a servant church encouraging the priesthood of the whole people of God.

I think the introduction of structures to facilitate growth will also mean a greater emphasis on the sacramental life of the church and on encouraging an apostolic spirituality. The church will become much more a house of prayer and a centre for teaching, service to the community and celebration. It will be in smaller groups, either within the liturgy or in people's homes, that people will learn to pray together, to break open the Word of God and to practise the mutual love and service which is the heart of a gospel life. I would also hope that the home would become a centre for liturgical life as we rediscover our Jewish heritage and experience being church as a daily reality, not just a Sunday duty.

There is much to be done!

Example

In the very first phase of becoming a missionary church St Mary's had adopted a cell structure and encouraged everybody in their congregation to attend one meeting a month for ongoing growth. The two new Christians who had been through the nurture course joined the group that their sponsors went to. This became the place where they could grow in their understanding of the faith and in fellowship. It was also the place where they could begin to think about the apostolic life and discover that they too had a responsibility to share the gospel with others.

As the church grew larger over the next few years new cells had to be created, and sometimes a group doing the nurture course could naturally become a new cell for growth. Tensions arose in the church. The priest found he was no longer able to remember easily the name of everyone in the congregation, and the intimacy and warmth that had so characterised their worship when there were about fifty people were noticeably lacking when there were over a hundred. It felt really good to be in a growing church, but it was not without its problems, and he was beginning to feel more and more stressed. He thought the answer lay in getting a curate, but the bishop made it clear that this option wasn't available. Actually, the answer lay in developing new structures for pastoral care. The cells took on more responsibility to look out for one another, and those who were not in cells – about half the congregation – were visited by a lay visiting team. The expectations of this 'one another care' were basic (making sure everyone in the church was visited by another member at least once a year and making sure that everyone was contacted if they missed more than the odd Sunday) but it made a huge difference, not least to the priest. He felt his role was changing, but as he was able to let go of some front-line pastoral responsibilities, so he was able to devote more time to developing lay leadership in other areas, and to using his own particular gifts to the full. The young woman whose awkward questions had so helped them at the beginning of their journey was employed as a part-time youth worker. The work with young people was beginning to take off and the youth group was slowly turning into a youth service and a youth congregation. The young people had been encouraged to create the worship themselves. It had begun as a slot at the end of their meeting but now it had overtaken them. Its reflective and contemplative style not only fed their own spiritual journey, but became something to which they invited others. As this ministry developed the youth worker started expressing a sense of vocation to the priesthood. Explorations began into her becoming an Ordained Local Minister. This was a way of supporting the growth of the church and particularly its ministry with young people.

Slowly the church developed structures through which growth could be sustained. The services on Sunday were becoming large celebrations with a strong family emphasis, owing to the growing numbers of children now attending through the after-school club, but the cell groups and a varied pattern of other worship were providing for the other needs of spiritual growth and a sense of belonging. Once a month they had an 'Adult Sunday School' happening before the Eucharist. This proved a good way of drawing into growth some who had never been involved in the cells.

As the spiritual temperature slowly rose, so the change was evident in people's lives. Morale was higher than it had ever been, and this over-flowed in service to the community and in evangelism. One of the first people to become a Christian started a small 'Agnostics Anonymous' discussion group during lunchtime at work. When asked why she had started it, she quoted Peter who, when warned to stop telling people about Jesus replied, 'we cannot keep from speaking about what we have seen and heard' (Acts 4:20).

9

EVANGELISING WORSHIP

IN HIS TYPICALLY COLOURFUL and provocative treatise on worship Richard Giles makes this appeal:

> If we can imagine a whole liturgy – not just a homily – that disrupts as much as it consoles, that offers us alternative images, that reshapes the way we imagine, that enables us to react violently against the forces, internal and external, that enslave us, then we shall be on the way to a new state of seeing and being. Perhaps also we shall no longer need to ask questions about why the Church has lost its way and speaks no longer to the young.[1]

In another passage he quotes Annie Dillard, who says,

> it is madness to wear ladies' straw hats to church; we should all be wearing crash helmets. Ushers should issue life preservers and signal flares; they should lash us to our pews. For the sleeping God may wake someday and take offence, or the waking God may draw us out to where we can never return.[2]

Such is the power of worship. Be careful what you pray for: it will be answered.

This chapter explores three inter-related issues:

* how we let the gospel shape our worship afresh
* how worship can itself be a means of evangelism
* how the culture in which we are set encourages us to find fresh ways of expressing Christian community and worship.

WORSHIPPING WELL

In my ministry over the past fifteen years as missioner and in the past year as bishop I have worshipped in hundreds of churches. There is no nice way of putting this, but the worship in many churches of a central to catholic tradition feels tired and lifeless. In part, this is the fault of buildings that were never meant for the kind of worship we want to put on today. And the current mediocrity is sometimes aggravated by small worshipping communities that are resistant to change and wedded to a certain form of worship. But there is also a lack of leadership and a lack of nerve, a lowering of expectations and a dearth of examples of really good ways of worshipping differently. There also seems to be a surprising lack of teaching about the principles of worship beyond the study of liturgical texts. Ironically, *Common Worship* hasn't helped here. Although it has hugely increased our knowledge of liturgical principles, it has unintentionally created a generation of priests who seem to think that planning worship involves sitting in front of a computer screen producing booklets. Not enough creative thought is going into the space we occupy, the experiences we sense, and the actions that will speak louder than the words. To quote again from Richard Giles,

> In reality, liturgical renewal involves the creation of a whole new way of doing liturgy, a process of transformation whereby the community of faith arrives at a place where it sees and understands everything it says and does in a totally new light. No text, however poetic or inspired, can carry the weight of this task by itself.[3]

The real meaning of the word 'liturgy' is not 'words on a page', but 'the work of the people'. Worshipping God is supposed to be the response of the whole Christian community using all its gifts, all its senses and all its skills.

I write here, not as a liturgical scholar, but as a jobbing priest whose work is the ordering of worship. When we plan worship, what we believe about ourselves as those who are united in Christ should shape what we do. The action and experience of our liturgy ought to reflect what we believe and ought to provide the most basic statement about our belief: a kind of shop window into all that is good and lovely about the Christian faith; indeed, a window into heaven. So here are my priorities for evangelising worship, and I offer them as a quick way into re-thinking how we plan what we do.

1. The space

Imagine someone coming to worship. The first thing they experience is the building itself, its appearance and its layout. Is it welcoming? Does it speak clearly of what we are going to do? Is it comfortable? Is it warm? Before they have even reached the door they will have seen a noticeboard which nine times out of ten is riddled with Christian jargon that is fairly unintelligible to anyone not initiated into church culture and often incorrect anyway. (Why can't we just say the church meets for worship at 10.30 and all are welcome? Also, saying what time it finishes and what happens if you bring children might also be more useful than words like 'Eucharist' or 'Matins'.)

Visitors then need to find the way in – literally and metaphorically. Where is the door? And how many other doors are there that might have to be tried first? And who will talk to them and help them find their way around?

Of course, this is where we bump straight into the constraints of so many church buildings. They are often old and expensive to keep and unsuited to our needs. Nevertheless, there is much that can be done, either by creating a space within the building where a different way of worshipping can be developed, or through re-ordering the whole building. I also wonder whether too many communities lack the nerve to find a way of making the building work in the way they desire, treating it as their master not their servant. Whether we like it or not, the layout and appearance of our buildings will speak volumes to those who join us for worship. If the noticeboard is out of date, if the entrance is piled with junk, if it isn't actually clear where the entrance is, if the carpet is threadbare, and if the congregation of thirty is spread among the back five pews of a building that can seat 200 and no one sits next to anyone else, then this will tell its all-too-obvious story. We need to have a bolder vision. There is much we could do to improve our worship space without necessarily having to spend anything except effort and imagination. An up-to-date noticeboard, clear signs, a removal of clutter will all make a big difference. And if you have got some money to spend, seats will always be better than pews. They are more comfortable and more flexible. They can be taken out and put in as required, changing the mood of the space and setting the scene for worship.

Catholic worship has a keen eye for symbol and space, and the particular artefacts we use in our worship should sit in their own particular space and be allowed to speak of their purpose clearly. There should really only be one altar in a church, the place where we gather for the Eucharistic meal, and if at all possible the altar table should be clearly visible and there should be a sense in which we gather round it. The font should not be sitting next to the altar, crowding its space, but in a place of its own and best of all close to the door, signalling its purpose as entry into the church. Next to it stands the paschal candle symbolising the presence of the Risen Christ. The lectern – the place of the Word – should also have its own space and the Bible should be open upon it for here God's Word is spoken to the assembled church. If the sacrament is reserved, and if the holy oils are kept, they too should have their spaces, perhaps in a side chapel reserved for prayer. But the church itself is not the building, nor the things in it, but the people who assemble to worship. Therefore, even if we are meeting in a hall or someone's home, we should think carefully about how we arrange the space so that it reflects what we are about and creates a warm and welcoming environment.

Little things can also make a big difference. I know a church which just put some dimmer switches on the lights. For a tiny cost the mood and feeling of the building and the worship could be altered. Re-ordering a side chapel so as to create a different kind of space for worship can be the first step towards a much bigger and bolder re-use of the building.

Richard Giles' book *Re-pitching the Tent* is an invaluable guide for churches that want to explore the possibilities of re-ordering and carefully evaluate how they use their space. I don't know a single church that having embarked on this journey is not enormously thankful for the benefits it has brought, not just to its worship but to the whole use of the building within the community.

2. The pictures

Next we need to ask, what will visitors see when they enter the church, or when they take their seat, and throughout the worship? Catholic worship should be visual and sensuous. There should be pictures and statues that arrest our vision and demand our attention.

For several years I served as a priest in Chichester. It is impossible to go into that great cathedral without being confronted by the paintings, tapestries and stained glass of some of the finest artists of the past fifty years. An ancient place becomes also a contemporary place, eloquently providing continuity and relevance between the present and the past. I often used to stand and look at the Piper tapestry behind the high altar and eavesdrop on the comments that visitors made. No one was unaffected by its contemporary vision and no one could leave thinking the Christian faith belonged only to the past. Similarly in Peterborough Cathedral, where I served for two years, the great crucifix which hangs in the nave draws the attention of all who visit, and challenges for a response.

We live in a visual culture where people are sophisticated in their understanding of visual language. Images are important, so this is not only a sphere which connects with the world around us but is also one in which catholic spirituality can contribute to the rest of the Church. But our heritage does need examining and developing. Too many pictures and statues are sentimental and uninspiring. Some churches are bare, with no visual impact at all. Others are full of clutter where nothing is allowed to speak for itself. The seasons of the church year provide an opportunity for change and variety. We should also be thinking about how we can commission new works of art, possibly inviting schools and colleges to help us. And daring to get rid of those that don't work anymore.

Modern technology opens up new possibilities to include the visual in our liturgy. Projected images or video clips now enhance worship in many different ways, either commentating on the action of the liturgy, providing stimulus for meditation or illustration for preaching. Charismatic and evangelical churches lead the way here, but it is an area in which churches of a catholic tradition should feel naturally at ease and there is so much we could do to enrich our liturgy. As we rethink our worship space and re-order our buildings we need to make sure we are able to erect screens large enough for people to see so that we can make the most of modern technology to give visual impact to our liturgy. A PowerPoint projector is now a basic piece of kit that every church should own. Such technology can complement the more traditional use of pictures and statues.

Then, of course, there is the visual impact of the furnishings themselves and of the robes and vestments the priest wears. All these things tell a story and, at the very least, even if we feel powerless to make the changes we desire, we should ask what it is that they are saying to our visitors and try, as far as possible, to let them speak clearly of a faith which is both ancient and forever new.

3. The welcome

I have already mentioned the importance of the welcome, but it cannot be stressed too much: more than the hymns, the sermon, the fragrance of the incense or the beauty of the building, the person coming to church for the first time will remember the welcome. This begins at the entrance to the church and continues throughout the service until the person leaves. Those who have responsibility for handing out the books (unhelpfully called 'sidesmen' in the Church of England) need to re-imagine their duties as ministers of welcome. Giving out the books is the least important thing they do. Sensitively welcoming people is the most important.

Bob Jackson puts it this way:

> Churches that grow tend to be those that have a welcoming front door that is wide enough to walk through. The job of welcome entails finding each newcomer several friends within the first few weeks. This is the centrepiece of any contemporary evangelism strategy, for these days people tend to belong before they believe. Many need to experience the reality of Christian community before they can accept the reality of Christ's presence within it. The love of God is discovered in the love of his people. Normally this welcoming into the community needs to be done by a team of lay people. It cannot be the vicar's job because, increasingly, the paid clergy are covering a multiplicity of churches and services, and leaving it to the vicar restricts the absorptive capacity of the church.[4]

These words echo so much that we have explored elsewhere in this book. They emphasise again that the hospitality of God is the motivation and the proper expression of our evangelism. But there are other aspects of our worship which can also be used to express welcome.

Common Worship identifies the first part of the Eucharist as 'The Gathering'. This description itself acknowledges that a worshipping community is gathered together and doesn't just happen. We also need to recognise that we bring to the service all that has happened to us in the week before. All this needs acknowledging. Indeed, many people arrive at church having just had a row with their partner or child about the very fact of coming at all. Sometimes a short notice can be given before the service begins, explaining to any newcomers basic bits of information for navigating their way through the liturgy, but also providing space for people to acknowledge some of the stuff they are bringing with them. In some way the church needs to demonstrate that it realises that its worship cannot be disconnected from the world around. Inviting people to be silent for a minute or two before the service begins can be the best way of doing this.

In the Eucharist, the opening rites of greeting, preparation and penitence also enable people to enter into the worship of God: not leaving things behind, but allowing them to be reconfigured within the embrace of Christian community and faith. Hearts and minds are made ready, sins are acknowledged, forgiveness assured. Then there is the great praise of the *Gloria* in which our voices are joined with the song of heaven.

But the welcome still goes on. Newcomers will need help finding the right page, and all the worshipping community share responsibility for providing this help. If there are children present they need to be welcomed into whatever children's liturgy or crèche is taking place, and if there is no provision of this sort (which there should be), then at least there should be books and appropriate toys available somewhere. The Diocese of Wakefield was instrumental in pioneering what have become known as 'pew bags', containing toys and books with a biblical or seasonal theme and available for small children to play with and enjoy during the service.

And at the end of the service, and especially if people stay for coffee, they still need welcoming, and some members of the congregation need to know it is their responsibility to look out for newcomers and talk to them. Too many first-time visitors to church will tell you that everyone was very friendly and smiley (sometimes too much so) when they arrived, but at coffee afterwards the regular congregation, cocooned in their holy huddles, avoided them like the plague.

4. The dance

Worship is a participative drama. Although some of us may have had the rather disconcerting experience of attending some avant-garde Brechtian drama and, having thought we were members of the audience, discovered we were members of the cast, this is always the case with all worship.

There are no spectators. The need for all to participate begs questions of the way we order our buildings, where so much of the action seems to take place on a 'stage' at the front, with only a few players having any significant part to play. All are involved in the drama of liturgy, because worship is about our communion with God. No one can do this on our behalf. While we may not all have the gift or calling for a specific ministry within the liturgy, all of us are involved by our presence and participation. Liturgy is the people's work. Usually we think of this participation only in terms of what we say and sing, but the layout of the building and our movement within it is one of the most dramatic ways we give expression to the truths we experience in worship; that we are made for community with God. David Stancliffe quotes this rather lovely observation from a four-year-old: 'Now I know why churches are true; the people in them enjoy singing and walk about in patterns.'[5] It is very important to get these patterns – the movement of our worship – right. I am calling this 'the dance of worship', and it involves us thinking again about the space we occupy and how we journey round it.

Think of the Eucharist as an encounter. In traditional catholic ceremonial there are three kisses: the priest kisses the altar at the beginning of Mass; after the Book of the Gospels is read, it is kissed; and we greet each other with a kiss at the Peace. These three kisses map out a Eucharistic theology of encounter. We encounter Jesus at the altar in bread and wine. We encounter Jesus in the Bible. We encounter Jesus in each other. He is present in Word and sacrament and in his body, the Church. The movement and ritual of our worship should emphasise these encounters.

We begin as a gathered community, sitting together in one place. If there is to be a separate liturgy of the Word for children (and please lets get rid of the term 'Sunday School' altogether – we come to church to worship, not to be educated!), it should begin *after* we have gathered, the children being sent out from the worshipping community to explore God's Word in a way that is appropriate for them, and then welcomed back at the Peace where we again express our belonging to each other.

After the Gathering Rite the first part of the Eucharist is the Liturgy of the Word. Here we gather around what is sometimes called 'the table of the Word'. Scripture is read and broken open so that we can hear God speaking to us afresh and allow our lives to be led and shaped by his Word. There is no reason why this should always be done passively: one person reading, everyone else listening. We don't consider this to be the best way for children to engage with God's Word, so why is it different for adults? As I mentioned earlier in connection with extending the Eucharist as a way of helping people grow in their faith, so exploring different ways of breaking open God's Word could also become part of the Sunday pattern of worship.

The Liturgy of the Sacrament begins with the sharing of Peace. As I have already indicated, the Peace is one of the high points of the Eucharist. Having heard Jesus speak to us through his Word and in preparation to receive him through the sacrament of his Body and Blood, we now turn to each other and greet his presence among us.

Some liturgical writers have suggested that one of the best ways we can enjoy and appropriate these different encounters, and the movement between them, is by actually getting up and moving. This is particularly emphasised by Richard Giles in the book I quoted from earlier, *Creating Uncommon Worship*. The idea is that we gather in one part of the building – perhaps even in a separate room – to break open the Word and then, after we have shared the Peace, move to another space to break open the bread. This gathering and moving and gathering again and being sent out gives focus to the different parts of the service, but also emphasises the whole movement of the Christian life. Nourished by God's Word and sacrament, and in community with Christian brothers and sisters, we journey on. We are gathered to God's Word and God's table; but we are also sent out from it to share what we have received.

This movement in the worship was commonplace in St Thomas', Huddersfield, where Richard Giles was the vicar and where I served and worshipped for eight years. At Peterborough Cathedral where we began a Saturday evening Eucharist we developed a similar pattern. This was an evangelistic Eucharist and we found that the movement through the building was one of many ways that we were able to draw newcomers into the pattern of our worship.

We can see this Eucharistic pattern and this movement in the Emmaus Road story. The disciples travel with Jesus and he explains the Scriptures to them. They sit down and eat with him and he is known in the breaking of bread. They are turned around and rush back to Jerusalem to share their experience.

Other ancient ceremonies of the Church also give emphasis to these encounters. Where incense is used, it marks out the altar, the Scriptures and the priest and people as holy. Candles are placed upon the altar and around the Bible. Responses to greet the reading of the Gospel and to accompany the Eucharistic Prayer are often sung.

There are also the particular movements and gestures made by the priest and by others who have defined roles in the worship. All these need to be carefully considered. Even how the priest holds his or her hands at the altar will communicate crucial things to all who are worshipping. Are the palms facing out as if to say 'Keep out' or 'Stay away', or are they beckoning the people to join in? Or are they perhaps held empty before God and waiting to be filled? And why shouldn't the whole congregation hold out their hands in this classical position of prayer during the action of the Eucharist? Although it is the priest who says the Eucharistic Prayer, the congregation are not spectators. There are responses to sing and actions to be made: the sign of the cross; genuflection; hands held aloft in praise – all these need to be taught and understood so that people can enter into the worship with their whole being.

Then, on certain occasions, there are dramatic actions that can give special emphasis to what is being celebrated. The liturgies of Holy Week and Easter are full of opportunities for movement and ceremony within the worship. In Huddersfield, as well as the traditional ceremonies of foot-washing, a watch of prayer, adoration of the cross, the new fire at dawn on Easter Day and the blessing of water in the font, we also used to dance. After Communion on Easter morning the whole congregation would join in a kind of country dance around the altar. It was a wonderfully joyful way of greeting the Risen Christ. I recently attended worship at Hilfield Friary on a Sunday morning. The invitation to gather around the table for the Eucharistic Prayer involved a simple dance to gather us together. The same simple steps – which only took us a few minutes to learn before the service – were used to send us out at the dismissal.

These suggestions won't be appropriate for every church. Each worshipping community needs to pay attention to the choreography of its worship and develop a style that is clearly part of the worship of the one Church but authentic to that community, developing those patterns that will serve it best.

Then there are the things that could happen at every service and engage people on other levels, such as sprinkling with holy water to accompany the prayer of absolution, or using lighting and candles more dramatically, and burning incense on a more regular basis, especially on the great festivals of the church year. Far from being irrelevant to the culture of our day it is these very things that speak of mystery, movement and wonder which draw people in. If they are also accompanied by images and music that connect with people (and if the welcome is right), then this will be worship that attracts.

In a council estate parish where I once served, the only service to which young people from the estate, who regularly used to hang out around the church, would actually come to join in the worship was Benediction on Sunday evening. It was the silence, the incense, the candles – the feeling of mystery – that drew them.

Right at the heart of the Eucharist is action. As well as encounter the Eucharist is also parable. At the Last Supper Jesus acts out with bread and wine what will happen to his body on the cross. It will be broken and his blood will be shed. He asks his friends to do this to remember him. For the Jews, to remember meant to make present. The Jewish Passover is not a passive recollection of an historic event, but a participation in God's saving acts. The same is true of the Christian Eucharist: as Jesus commanded we take bread and wine; we break it and pour it out; we share it. There are words that accompany these actions, and they are important because they enshrine our theology of the cross as much as they do our theology of the Eucharist, for in sharing bread and wine we share Christ's victory over sin and death. But the actions speak louder.

At the end of Graham Greene's novel *Monsieur Quixote*, the priest, deprived of his ministry and languishing in jail, celebrates the Eucharist without altar, without vessels, without bread, without wine and without words. He goes through the actions and enjoys Holy Communion.

At the very least all priests should be encouraged to think carefully about the drama of the liturgy and to take great care about how the actions speak and what they say. But we also need to think creatively about how our fuller sense of the whole church celebrating the Eucharist encourages further action and movement to enhance our worship.

We could call the movement and action of worship the body language of the church. Just as in conversation, facial expression and hand gesture will say as much, if not more, than the words, so it is with worship. The whole body speaks by all that it does.

5. The music

There is probably more controversy about the subject of music in church than any other. Indeed, some clergy have cynically reflected that they could stand up in church, deny their faith and denounce their God, but as long as they introduced no new hymns their ministry would be accepted.

It is unlikely that new people coming to church will know any of the music. Knowledge of hymnody in our society has reached a level where the only hymns you can be confident people know will be the few most famous Christmas carols, and clearly these cannot be sung on every Sunday of the year. Helping newcomers to feel at ease is again partly a matter of welcome, acknowledging that for people coming into the church most of what they experience will be alien and unknown. But the welcome also provides opportunity to introduce people to music and there is much to be gained by developing a simple repertoire of responsorial chants that can be learnt and picked up very easily. This was the sort of music we used at the Peterborough Saturday evening Eucharist for some parts of the service.

I also believe there is more room for musical variety than many churches care to admit. At St Nicholas' Church in Newbury, although they have a clear evangelical/charismatic ethos, they still honour a more Eucharistic and traditional inheritance and, alongside the main diet of worship-group-led songs and choruses, the choir still sings anthems. Indeed, in many ways the Eucharist feels like renewed catholic worship, a lovely example of God having shuffled the pack of our traditions and of the growing irrelevance of our labels. Most important of all, it works.

Many churches suffer because they are striving for a style of worship and a style of music that is inappropriate to their setting and their resources. There is no point trying to sing a Mozart Mass setting if you have no choir, and no point in a choir singing a complicated anthem if it is beyond their ability. And worship songs rarely work well with an organ, and so on. Honour and employ the gifts that God has given your congregation, aiming for a style that is your own. This will usually mean a variety of musical idioms, but a mix which is particular to your church, and one that will change as the church changes and grows.

6. The words

Almost at the end of our tour through the worship of the church we come to the words we say. I don't intend to say much about them. First, because it is an area with which clergy in particular are very familiar (indeed, many catholic clergy, as Jeffrey John observes, are obsessed by which rite and which text to use).[6] Second, because there are, in my view, more important things being neglected.

It is not that the words are unimportant. Indeed, for Anglicans they are particularly important since we claim no doctrine of our own, having received our faith from the wider Church. The words enshrine and define those beliefs and represent a particular Anglican spirituality and flavour. All this is very important. And the words are beautiful, and the recitation of text a pricelessly valuable aspect of worship, equipping people with a vocabulary that will serve their prayer throughout a lifetime and web them into a tradition of praise. Nevertheless, if we get all the aspects of worship I have talked about above right, it will matter less and less what particular texts we use. Doing what we do well, with a pleasant demeanour and with due attention to all the other things that make worship work, matters more than forever fiddling with the words. *Common Worship* has beguiled us with its huge range of options. I am making a pitch for clergy to understand that planning the worship means more than selecting texts. We should be familiar with the texts; and we should choose from the beautiful and varied range that *Common Worship* offers and find the ones that will best fit our situation, but, as with so many things, less is more. We should value the silence between the words as much as the words themselves, always remembering that other parts of the liturgy are speaking more loudly.

We need to make sure those new to the church have the words they need in a form that is clear and accessible. People don't necessarily need all the words, just the ones they are saying. Especially during the Eucharistic Prayer we don't want people's heads buried in a book, but looking expectantly to the altar, attending to the action taking place.

It will also be helpful for the priest to learn some of the words by heart so that the body language of presiding is addressed to God and the assembled church rather than sideways to a book on the altar. 'The liturgy is a framework that you have to inhabit and make your own, so that you communicate through it. Don't make it a self-protective barrier.'[7]

7. The sending out

The word 'mass' and the word 'mission' both have the same Latin root, the word *missa*, from the verb *mittere*, to send out. The climax of the Eucharist is not Communion but being sent out to participate with God in his mission in the world. The Eucharist is not the hot bath at the end of the day, but the cold shower at the beginning. We go to church on Sunday to worship God (to be gathered in), but also to be guided and nourished in order to be sent out. This is why, in most cases, I think the best place for notices is after Communion and before the blessing and dismissal (note the same mission-centred word). They will be easier to remember at this point, but they also indicate a commissioning (that word again). As we go into the world, so we go about our business as a Christian community and the notices are the things to be brought to our attention. Also the words of dismissal should be the final words, spoken after the closing hymn. We could call this the fourth kiss – a kiss of life – as we are commissioned to be Christ's people. It is also the final movement of the Eucharist: out into the world.

Understanding the sending out as the climax of the Eucharist will also help shape the teaching and preaching that goes on within it. The priest should be chiefly concerned with helping people relate the faith they celebrate on Sunday to the life they lead on Monday, preparing people for heaven and preparing them for life.

EVANGELISTIC PREACHING

I seem to have written a whole book about evangelism, and now said a whole lot about worship, without once mentioning preaching. Partly this is because I want to move the church away from thinking of evangelism as a ministry that only belongs to the up-front preacher, and partly it is because in the kind of evangelism this book describes the message of the gospel will be communicated by example and by testimony, by explanation and most often through dialogue. And this is a ministry where all the baptised have a part to play. However, there is a still a vitally important place for preaching. In some evangelistic ministry, and in almost every act of worship, at some point there will be a sermon. And how people experience and perceive the Christian faith will, to a large extent, be based upon

their experience of that sermon. If you speak to most people coming out
of church and ask them whether they enjoyed the service, if they say yes,
it probably means they enjoyed the sermon and they knew the hymns.
Conversely, if they say no, it is because the preaching was dull and the
music duller. But the quality of the preaching is still a yardstick by which
the attractiveness of the Christian faith is measured,

I believe that the spoken word still has great power to move us, challenge us and change us. I don't believe that people's attention span has
shrunk to thirty seconds, or whatever it is that the latest research reports.
I do believe that the way people process spoken information has changed
and is changing, and therefore the way we communicate must change. But
I see thousands of people pay good money to listen to Eddie Izzard or
Billy Connolly talk for two hours non-stop: their ability to hold people's
attention beyond a few minutes is not in doubt. Consequently, the more
uncomfortable question the church needs to face is this: are our preachers
any good at it? But that is the subject for another book. Here I simply want
to affirm the importance of the ministry, and say a little about evangelistic preaching.

On most Sundays the preaching will be primarily concerned with building up the faith of the Christian community and relating that faith to daily
life. It will not be evangelistic or educational. Incidentally, I've never
thought the sermon a particularly good medium for teaching. There is
virtually no opportunity for interaction: hence my attraction to the concept
of 'long church'. This is where real learning can take place.

In some Sunday services – perhaps where there is a baptism and large
numbers of newcomers are present, or when the bishop comes to
confirm – there is a great opportunity to preach evangelistically. This calls
for a different style. The sermon is not just guiding and instructing people
in the faith they already hold, but inviting people who may know little or
nothing about the Christian faith to consider its claims. This sort of
preaching will probably be shorter, more personal, more anecdotal and
have as much the feel of a testimony as a sermon. Indeed you could do a
lot worse than studying Billy Connolly to get some idea of how this kind
of preaching might work. Notice that successful comedians nowadays do
not tell jokes. The joke is an old linear form, with a beginning, a middle
and a punchline at the end. The traditional sermon is similar, with its three
points to make, and its careful structure and its beginning, middle and end.
And it is usually written out and, however beautiful the prose, too often
delivered without much passion.

Comedians nowadays tell stories. They hold up a mirror to life, show
you how absurd it can be, and make you laugh. The evangelising preacher
is doing something similar. The preacher tells stories. We hold a mirror up
to life, show people how sacred it is, and lead them to worship. Or at least

we open people up to the possibility that this crazy, muddled world does contain goodness, hope, beauty and purpose. And the evangelistic preacher will do this by deliberately laying before the congregation something of his or her own experience of the Christian faith, giving some indication of the difference it makes and inviting people to explore it for themselves. This sort of sermon will usually be delivered from a few notes, rather than a full text, and with a conviction and passion that are too often lacking. Read about the great Anglo-Catholic priests of the nineteenth century and you will read about passionate preachers. We need to re-discover something of that zeal to communicate the gospel. We also need to recover confidence in the medium of preaching itself. It can still change lives, but this is not brought about by the eloquence or even the passion of the preacher, but through God's ability to take our words and use them in the hearts and minds of those who are seeking. Most preachers will have had the experience of someone coming up to them after their sermon and thanking them for something that they didn't actually say. What is happening here is two-fold. Their words have sparked a chain of thought within the listener that has led to some revelation. And the Holy Spirit has been at work anointing the offering of our sermon. But we do have our part to play, preparing a different sort of sermon for a different sort of need.

Most important of all, we need to pray that God may inspire and guide the preaching ministry of the church. As Ken Leech has observed:

> It is more important that the preacher has prayed, has been pierced by the word of God, and has become open to the activity of the spirit, than that she has made elaborate and tidy preparation. None of us knows how God is going to use us, and we shouldn't be too 'ready'.[8]

Need we quote this scripture again? 'From the abundance of the heart the mouth speaks.' So let us prepare our hearts for a ministry of preaching that can change us as well as those we speak to.

Alongside this sort of evangelistic preaching there can also be actual testimonies from members of the Christian community talking about their own experience of faith. This sort of thing doesn't usually happen in catholic parishes, but where it does I have known it make a huge difference. The parish where I served my title in South London regularly invited lay people to give testimony as part of the preaching ministry of the church – not instead of the sermon, but as a way of illustrating what the sermon was saying by using the example of the lives of those who had learned this lesson themselves. This sort of testimony was also used liturgically. In Holy Week members of the congregation spoke about their own experiences of living the Christian life as a way of punctuating the liturgy. For example, a nurse who worked in a local hospice spoke on Good Friday about her own being alongside those who were dying; what it meant for her life and how her faith resourced her. This sort of testimony is not only good in itself, but is a powerful way of communicating the truth and relevance of the Christian faith to those who are exploring. It cannot of itself persuade anyone to believe (but, of course, we are not in the persuasion business). But it can convince people of the reality of faith in that person's life in a way that raises questions for every person's life.

The best evangelistic preachers will also have this impact. The preaching will have a certain uncomfortable directness. 'This is what I have found to be true in my own life', the preacher will be saying. 'And if you have questions like this in your life, then I can't persuade you to believe the same as I believe, but I can invite you, and even implore you, to take the risk of finding out more and exploring the way of life that is offered to us in Jesus Christ.'

CAN THE EUCHARIST EVANGELISE?

So far all that has been said is based on the assumption that the main service will be the Eucharist. Of course, in many churches this will not be the case. But I have spoken intentionally about the Eucharist because, as well as it being the main service in most catholic parishes, I firmly believe it to be evangelistic. I simply don't buy the attitude that says the Eucharist is not appropriate for people who are new to church.

First of all, the Eucharist is the one service given to us by Jesus himself. It is one of the greatest treasures of the Church. In receiving the bread and wine of Holy Communion we receive the life of Jesus: the fruits of his dying and rising are made available to us.

Secondly, and of more practical relevance, *all* church services are strange and alien to those who have never worshipped before. There simply isn't a way of doing it that will be immediately credible and nor should there be. One of the great mistakes the Church of England has made in recent years is to muddle accessibility and credibility. Of course we make our services as accessible as possible, and, as I have already made clear, this will be much more about the welcoming environment we provide than any of the things we do or say in the service. But if we sacrifice the necessary *incredibility* of our claims and try to make our faith instantly understandable, then the baby will be lost with the bath water. For the new person, holding up a piece of bread and proclaiming, 'This is the Lamb of God who takes away the sins of the world' will be as mystifying and unintelligible as waving arms in the air and singing 'Forever he will be the Lamb upon the throne'. As this book has been at pains to point out, evangelism must begin where people are and accompany them to Christ. Therefore, for most people, much will have happened *before* they come to church in our places of nurture. But, even for those who do come through the door without another contact, what will impress them will be the warmth of our welcome and the authenticity of what we do.

For catholic Christians there is nothing more authentic and nothing which shapes our life more than our participation in the Eucharist. We should not be embarrassed to invite people to join us around the Lord's Table and we must shape the way we celebrate the Eucharist so that it includes people. 'We ought to be able to say with confidence,' writes David Stancliffe, 'share with us the breaking of the bread, and you will see Christ crucified among his people, forming them as his Body; and this feast will give you a glimpse of heaven...worship, and the Eucharistic worship which is at the centre of Catholic life and practice, offers us a pattern where welcome and belonging leads us to a deepening relationship with Christ and forms us as a people on the way.'[9]

For some, the particular problem is Communion itself. This sacrament which is the sign of our inclusion is inevitably a sign of exclusion for those who don't receive. However, it is my experience that if a proper explanation is given, then there is no reason why people should feel anything but admiration for the commitment they witness. Holy Communion is something to look forward to as a sign of our commitment and belonging to Christ. It is not that we wish to turn anyone away, but long for all to come freely. Also, the offer of a blessing is a real and tangible expression of our desire to include people in a way that is appropriate to their receiving of faith. Moreover, I can think of many people who, having made the journey to faith and regularly received a blessing, find that after they started receiving Communion they miss the touch and intimacy of blessing.

Having said this, there are real theological questions about who should or shouldn't receive Communion. I have always welcomed all who love Christ and who would normally receive Communion in their church to feel welcome to receive, and would never interrogate anyone at the altar rail and ask for credentials! But in the Gospels we find Jesus welcoming all to his table, especially those whom others would exclude. There is an irony that in the Church of England we tend to ring-fence the table and offer an open font. In the New Testament the reverse is true. As we begin to encourage children to receive Communion, and learn how to welcome them and prepare them for this wonderful sacrament, perhaps we will learn more of how to welcome everyone.

Neither should we draw the conclusion that catholic parishes should have the Eucharist and nothing else. The Eucharist will always be at the heart of the church, but there are other ways of worshipping that will also be helpful to draw and accompany others in.

I have already mentioned the power and attraction of services such as Benediction or other occasions which are based around reflection and silence. Many Roman Catholic communities are re-discovering a service of the Word through a lay-led Office of Morning or Evening Prayer, sometimes as a main service of the week.

I heard recently of some Anglican churches in central New York where on Friday and Saturday evenings at around 10.00 or 11.00 the doors have been thrown open, and the choir have sung Benedictine chant in the candle-lit church and waited to see what would happen. And people have come. They have been drawn to the authentic voice of worship beckoning from a sacred space. This will not be a strategy that many can follow: but how about some of our cathedrals and city-centre churches throwing open their doors in such a way? Many nightclubs now have 'chill-out zones' where people go to mediate and relax and often some sort of so-called spiritual and meditative music is played. Some of our churches could provide such a space. It embodies a faith whose first word is welcome and whose roots are deeply planted in a living tradition.

EVANGELISING THROUGH WORSHIP

This brings us to the subject of how we evangelise *through* worship. If we return to that basic question we asked ourselves a couple of chapters ago – how can we serve the people with whom we have contact in such a way that the gospel is intriguing, challenging and appealing? – and as we think again about some of the individuals and groups of people with whom we have contact and what sort of event they might attend, we find our minds turning to worship. For many people worship events can be a way into faith. This is partly a consequence of living in an age where there is such a great fascination with all things spiritual, but it is also because all human beings have a longing within them to mark great events in their lives with a seriousness that takes them outside themselves. Hence, many couples still want to be married in church, most people still want some sort of religious burial and a lot of people still want their children baptised. Their desire does not necessarily spring from a specific Christian faith, but because the secular alternatives seem empty and there is a longing within them for something else. These rites of passage provide great opportunity for the church and at their centre is a liturgical celebration – an act of worship – which needs to be prepared for and conducted in a way that connects with people's longings and communicates Christian faith. This can be evangelism through worship. But there are other opportunities, large and small, for worship to be evangelistic.

First of all there are the occasions which arise naturally through the year. The evangelistically minded church will pay great attention to the seasons of the year seeing there natural opportunities to gather people together and celebrate faith. These are the Christingles, crib services, Mothering Sunday celebrations and Pentecost 'birthday-party-for-the-church' services that punctuate the Christian year. All Souls' Day provides an opportunity to invite all the bereaved of the past year to come and remember their loved ones. Holy Innocents' Day provides an opportunity to minister to families whose children have died (this was a small but intensely beautiful service we started in Peterborough Cathedral). St Francis-tide is an opportunity to have a pets' service. And so on. Look through the year and see the opportunities to bring people together. The new service book *Times and Seasons* provides resources for many of these services, as does *Patterns for Worship*. We have a rich supply of liturgical material.

Then there are what I call the 'creative one-offs'. There can never be a strategy for such events since, by definition, they cannot be repeated, but they offer a strategic approach to worship and evangelism. We need to keep our evangelistic antennae out for what is happening in the community and respond creatively. A good example from when I served in Yorkshire in the early 1990s, and at a time when many coal mines were being closed, was a church which put on a requiem for the pit. In the same way that there can only be one funeral when a person dies, so with the death of the pit, which was in so many ways the heart of the community. The church provided a space and a ritual for people to bring their grief and cry out to God and draw together in seeking hope in their bereavement. I know of other churches that in times of national crisis, such as the recent war in Iraq, or following terrorist atrocities, have put on one-off services of prayer and found people welcoming a place to gather and give expression to their concern. All of us will have noted how people still turn to the church at these times and we can make a very positive contribution by anticipating this need, opening our churches and, where appropriate, putting on services that will provide the space that people long for. This too is evangelistic.

Linked in with this are the possibilities for evangelism which arise as a result of the search for spiritual truth that is going on in so many people today. Offering opportunities for people to learn to pray or to experience a new approach to prayer can be one of the best ways of making and developing contacts with those who are seeking after spiritual truth but who are not yet ready either to explore Christian faith or join Christian worship. In Peterborough Cathedral I was involved in several initiatives that sought to gather people together who wanted to deepen their spirituality but who were still quite a long way from Christian commitment.

On Sunday evenings there was a group called 'Praying with your whole being' which is best described as Christian yoga. Using the insights and practice of yoga the woman who ran the group as it were 'baptised' this popular and meaningful way of meditating and, using Christian prayer and certain biblical texts, enabled people to enter into a way of prayer and meditation that used their whole body and whole person. It was extremely popular.

On Saturday mornings the same woman laid out in the north transept of the cathedral a labyrinth she and her husband had painted onto a huge canvas. People were invited to walk the labyrinth and meditate on the course their journey was making or on the way they were travelling through life. There were no particular instructions other than to walk and reflect, but aids to prayer – such as offering a stone that could be laid down at the centre of the labyrinth as a sign of relinquishing a burden or a flower placed as a sign of joy – were available. As well as finding that the labyrinth appealed to cathedral visitors, we found that people started coming to the cathedral specifically to walk it.[10]

There is now quite a widespread interest in labyrinths and prayer stations as a way of engaging with the culture around us. A Grove booklet is available on the subject.[11] There is also a six-week course called *Essence*, which is written for today's spiritual seekers'.[12] While at Peterborough, I led a group at the Adult Education Centre on Christian prayer and meditation encouraging people from outside the Christian community to gather at a neutral venue to have an opportunity to explore the Christian spiritual tradition.

All these ideas – and there must be many more – show how we can begin to satisfy the spiritual hunger we find in our society and reveal that the spiritual riches that make up the Christian tradition and are particularly cherished within the catholic tradition are the very things that people are longing to discover and experience.

THE MINISTRY OF HEALING AND RECONCILIATION

In the New Testament the proclamation of God's love and purpose is often accompanied by the signs and wonders of his healing power. In our out-reach offering prayer for healing and the chance for reconciliation will be powerfully attractive to those on the fringes of the Christian community and those outside it. These sacramental ministries of grace can be pro-foundly evangelistic. In Peterborough Cathedral the second largest congregation we had in our monthly cycle of worship was our Wednesday lunchtime healing service. It wasn't unusual for as many as a hundred people to gather to pray for healing and receive the laying on of hands. Many churches have found that regularly offering this sort of liturgy can not only be a blessing in itself but provide a way in for those who are lonely or broken. Prayer for healing can also be an invitation to know Christ the healer. The 'Pastoral Services' section of *Common Worship* offers a rich resource of material to help put together an appropriate liturgy. In my experience it is very important that such services include opportunity for individual prayer for healing and reconciliation. In most communities offering healing services should be part of a holistic strategy for evangelism which links pastoral care, worship and outreach.

FRESH EXPRESSIONS OF CHURCH

Finally, we need a strategy for evangelism that looks to plant fresh expressions of Christian community into the many networks of our society. For many people who come to faith on our nurture courses, and for even more who are outside of their reach, a different way of expressing church, perhaps taking place at a different time and in a different place, will present our best chance of engaging them with the truths of the gospel. The report *Mission-shaped Church*[13] has encouraged this sort of thinking, and although there is the danger of it becoming a bandwagon which will only end up re-branding what we already do so that every parent and toddler group now becomes a fresh expression of church, there is much to be gained by considering how to reach a group of people by establishing some sort of witnessing presence where they are. In time this witness will turn to worship. Indeed it may begin as worship since it is spirituality and resources for living that many people crave.

Currently most of the examples of mission-shaped church tend to come from evangelical churches but there are some exceptions. For example Fr Damian Feeney planted a Sunday Mass in the Asda supermarket in his parish.[14] In Ascot a curate has started a service she calls 'mini-mass': this is a Eucharist for parents and toddlers where all participate. At All Saints, Wokingham there is a non-Eucharistic but definitely liturgical service, again pioneered by the curate, that gathers together those for whom church has never been easy. They have developed a liturgical way of worshipping that expresses their journeying towards faith.

In the centre of Reading, St Laurence's, a community committed to building church with the kind of young people usually alienated from church culture, is finding ritual, movement and mystery vital ingredients in their outreach and is developing forms of worship which transcend the usual catholic and evangelical divides. It is a real liturgy (i.e. 'work of the people') as the young people themselves are shaping a way of worshipping that makes sense to them. The experience of this church reflects much that has happened in what is sometimes called 'alternative worship' being pioneered by Christian communities who are trying to create worship that is clothed in today's culture and speaking today's language. Many of these communities are finding that it is the symbolic, the sacramental, the mysterious and the intentionally ambivalent that are creating the kind of space and the kind of worship that many younger people can enter into.[15]

There is a re-discovery of catholic spirituality and worship going on in many of our churches and many of us haven't even noticed it! Catholic parishes need to wake up to the fact that it is the very aspects of our worship that some parts of the church have been telling us are irrelevant that are the ones that are speaking to young people today. It is not entertainment that young people crave, but holiness, authenticity and participation. These, surely, are the dance and feel of catholic liturgy.

But let me finish with a modest example from my own experience which is quoted (but un-attributed) in *Mission-shaped Church* and could be easily replicated in most parishes. When I became priest-in-charge of St Wilfrid's in Chichester I inherited a small midweek Eucharist. About ten people faithfully came each Wednesday morning. After about a year I noticed that a few new people had joined this congregation. One of them was an elderly woman who had recently come to faith and two were young mums with pre-school children. Whereas the other members of the congregation came on Sunday as well, these three only came on Wednesday. I visited them and chatted with them and tried to persuade them that they should come on Sundays (after all Sunday is proper church!), but they all had a good reason why this wasn't feasible. The older lady visited her family at weekends. The young mums found church and faith a battleground in their family. Neither of their husbands supported their churchgoing and one of them had an older child who played sports on Sunday mornings. After a little while the penny dropped. While I was fighting a rearguard action to keep Sunday special, the Holy Spirit had danced on ahead of me and was blessing Wednesdays. When I realised this, I started putting some resources into Wednesdays. We started singing hymns, I took more care over the preaching, and once a month we went back to the vicarage for a kind of housegroup for the Wednesday morning congregation. And it grew. Several years later, when I moved from the parish, it wasn't unusual to have a congregation of more than thirty people, a third of whom never came on Sunday.

When I moved to the Wakefield diocese I was involved in some research into patterns of church attendance. We asked one deanery to keep a register in every church over an eight-week period.[16] To our astonishment we found that only a small proportion of people came every week and there was a much larger number of one-off attenders than churches realised. Most interesting of all we found a missing congregation: these were the people who attended church regularly but never came on Sunday. In every church where they had regular weekday worship they had people attending who didn't come on Sundays. With the rapidly changing nature of Sunday in our culture this shouldn't really be surprising. What is surprising is that many churches still don't put on midweek worship of any sort. All the evidence suggests that we should have a greater diversity of times, as well as styles, of worship.

When I moved to Peterborough I was involved in putting on the monthly Saturday evening Eucharist mentioned earlier. This drew together a new congregation, especially appealing to families who had all sorts of other commitments on a Sunday morning, both work and leisure. In Wooton, a small village community just north of Abingdon, a non-Eucharistic, but definitely liturgical, Saturday evening service draws together a similar congregation and provides a way of worshipping that is accessible to those who are not used to church culture. Its friendly approach to church is summed up in the name: Saturday@Six. Much easier to relate to than the language we usually use to describe our worship.

We have to let go of the idea that there has to be one service in our churches which is the centre of our life and to which all people come. This concept has great theological integrity: the one people of God gathered around the one altar on a Sunday morning. However, if you have an eight-o-clock, you have already crossed the theological Rubicon. You have accepted that there can be *two* distinct worshipping communities under the umbrella of the one Christian community.

Sacramental theology has always taught us that there is really only one priest, Jesus Christ, and one Eucharist, in which all our other Eucharists combine: the one offering of the Son to the Father in which the voice of our praise is joined. Therefore all our Eucharists in all our churches foreshadow and participate in this one offering of thanksgiving. This principle of legitimate diversity which is enshrined in the geographic distinctions of our parish system now needs to be encouraged in the sociological distinctions of our complex society. We must plan for a greater diversity of expression in our worship, a greater diversity of time, and a greater diversity of venue, planting and creating church in the networks of people's lives and, as far as possible, in accordance with the different constraints and demands with which people are living. This must mean that alongside our Sunday Eucharist there will be other expressions of Christian and Eucharistic community developing. We should not see this as a concession to the spirit of the age – a kind of selling out to niche marketing – but as a Spirit-led evangelistic strategy whereby we reach out to those who do not yet know Christ with the greatest treasure we have to share: the gift of Christ himself in the Eucharist.

The church of the future will be more diverse than it is at present. It will therefore need to be more united. The Eucharist is the sacrament of our unity. Though we are many we are one body because we all share in the one bread. The Eucharist protects and conveys the unity we have in Christ. As we establish different worshipping communities we will need to pay careful attention to the bringing together of these communities so as to give proper expression to this deeper unity. Borrowing the language of the cell church movement: if we have cells we must also have celebrations. I think it is helpful to think of the freshly planted expressions of Christian community, worshipping in new ways and at different times, as cells of the church. The Sunday morning Eucharist is not the 'main service' that we hope the other cells will gravitate towards, but one cell among others; simply the one that has probably been around the longest, but not necessarily the one where there is the most potential for future growth. (That may be on Wednesday morning or Saturday evening.) Uniting all these different cells will be a larger and occasional service that will draw everyone together in a transcending celebration of Eucharistic community. In some rural and poorer urban areas, churches will best work together on this sort of strategy, the different churches of a deanery more consciously thinking of themselves as cells and therefore part of a closer organic unity with each other. Deanery celebrations will then express this closer belonging and this burgeoning diversity. In the Vale of the White Horse, the most rural deanery of my Episcopal Area, there are already signs of the individual parishes thinking more and more in this way. It is exciting to behold.

THE CONVERTING POWER OF WORSHIP

Worship converts. Why have we stopped believing this?

'The worshipping community, by its very worship and praise of God, attracts others into its midst, magnetises them, pulls them, sometimes against their will, to be part of this mysterious yet compelling activity', writes Richard Holloway.[17] 'If you don't worship you'll shrink; it's as brutal as that', declares the psychiatrist in Peter Shaffer's play *Equus*.[18] 'I can't escape the fact that the service was one of the most spiritually liberating experiences I've ever had', writes David le Jars.

> It wasn't because of the words, or the actions or the dogma. It was, I think, because of the underlying assumption of community. The sense that, in this fragmented society of ours, where the spiritual is perpetually being sidelined in favour of the material; where loving thy neighbour is something you do when the neighbour's husband is out at work; it's actually OK to be soulful.[19]

David le Jars is not a Christian. Worship seized him. 'It was the Church's worship that converted me', says David Stancliffe.[20] 'Come let us go up to the mountain of the Lord, to the house of the God of Jacob', cries the prophet Isaiah (Isaiah 2:3).

It seems particularly ironic that it is catholic parishes, whose heritage in the Church of England is built on social action and beautiful worship, that now lacks confidence that worship can be re-imagined and re-expressed in a way that will attract and convert. Does it say more about us and our own expectations of God than of the power of worship? Does it reflect our frustration with a society that seems less and less interested in Christian faith? Or are we in danger of diminishing God and imagining that his presence in worship can only be recognised by a few? 'We need forms of Christian community that are homes of generous hospitality, places of challenging reconciliation, and centres of attentiveness to the living God', says Brother Samuel SSF.[21]

I have already spoken about the fascination with all things spiritual that runs through our society. Let us take this as a signal that the tide is actually flowing in a catholic direction and that the treasures of our tradition are the very things for which the world hungers; and let us find ways of representing them afresh so that the world can be fed. This must involve a clear strategy for evangelism in the way that we have been exploring throughout this book, but it must also mean a renewed confidence in the gospel and a real desire to see the whole world shaped by the goodness and beauty of God. It also brings us back to where we started: have we received this as good news for ourselves, and if worship seems tired and lifeless to us who believe, well, what can we expect for others? Therefore let us work to renew the worship of our church and see worship as the wellspring for evangelism.

At the very beginning of this book there is a substantial quote from the Roman Catholic document on evangelism, *Evangelisation in the Modern World*. They are words to which I keep returning as I ponder on the call to evangelise. Let me quote some of them again. Speaking of the church the document says:

> The intimate life of this community – the life of listening to the Word and the Apostles' teaching, charity lived in a fraternal way, the sharing of bread – this intimate life only acquires its full meaning when it becomes witness, when it evokes admiration and conversion and becomes the preaching and proclamation of the Good News.[22]

They are astonishing words because they seem to be saying that all the things we treasure most within the Church – the Scriptures, the sacraments, our doctrines and beliefs, the Eucharist itself – only acquire their full meaning when they 'become witness', when they overflow into evangelism. It is as if we have not heard the Scriptures or received Communion until we have also sought to live the Scriptures and share our bread with others. This is worship and Christian life which is truly gathered in and sent out. It is worship that sustains and converts. The great Archbishop of Canterbury William Temple wrote of the converting power of worship in this beautiful way:

Worship is the submission of all our nature to God. It is the quick-
ening of conscience by his holiness; the nourishment of mind with
his truth; the purifying of imagination by his beauty; the opening of
the heart to his love; the surrender of will to his purpose – and all of
this gathered up in adoration, the most selfless emotion of which our
nature is capable and therefore the chief remedy from that self-
centredness which is our original sin and the source of all actual
sin.[23]

This is the worship that changes our lives and allows our lives to become
witness. As the hymn puts it: 'O come let us adore him!'

Example

For so many years St Mary's had totally overestimated what it could
achieve in the short term, and totally underestimated what it could achieve
in the long term. Initially change and growth had been slow. Then there
was a fairly rapid period of growth. And then a dip and a kind of plateau-
ing and consolidation before further growth. The Youth Worker was
ordained; a pattern of cell groups was established; a new approach to
Sunday morning was developed; a varied and sustainable pattern of evangelistic events, nurture courses, creative one-offs and new congregations
worshipping in different ways took root in the parish; and a leadership
team of lay and ordained people worked together to develop and oversee
this ministry. There were still problems. Two of the best leaders moved
house just as their ministry was really taking off. Some of the plans that
seemed to offer the greatest promise fell flat on their face. When the
diocese asked for more money, getting it to come in wasn't as hard as it
had been. Now, there was a feeling that people were giving to something
about which they felt ownership and pride. They were pleased to be part
of a growing church and they were pleased to support it realistically. There
was more talk about stewardship and less about money, but the money
came in. Sometimes it felt as if the growth was being taxed. It wasn't that
the church wasn't pleased to be supporting other parishes for the first time
in its history, rather than always expecting to be subsidised by someone
else, it was only that so few parishes seemed to have caught the vision for
growth and so few of them seemed to have any thought-through strategy
for evangelism. But when they were tempted to feel too pleased with
themselves, something usually came along to shake them up. And, of
course, there was always so much more they could be doing and so much
need in the community around them.

Ten years after their journey to become a missionary church had begun,
those regularly worshipping with them in their various congregations had
grown from about fifty to about 200. Of course, the regularity of

attendance was erratic and some fell away. By any account, however, this was fairly astonishing growth, and it was humbling to look back and see how it had all happened, particularly as for them it was not measured in numbers, but in people's lives: individuals who had been changed and a community which was now served by the church in a way that had probably not happened for centuries. And the most obvious and striking change was in the worship itself, not just the different services, but the feel of the worship and the hospitality of the community. Everyone commented on it. Clergy from other parts of the diocese even came to see what was going on, especially when the building was re-ordered. If only they could see that it was the re-ordering of the ministry that had really made the difference.

The bishop asked them to be a training parish and they got a curate just at the time they probably needed one the least. But this was now a parish where a new priest could learn about ministry in a missionary church. Her first Mass was a great occasion and a time of great celebration for the parish. During the Eucharistic Prayer a baby started crying. A loud, inconsolable sobbing filled the church, almost drowning out the music of the liturgy. Several people looked round, annoyance etched into their faces: shouldn't the mother take this baby out? The parish priest who had overseen all the change and growth smiled to himself. He was now only a year or so away from retirement: he had seen all this before and, however much they taught about welcome, there were always some people who wanted to place limits. He quietly went over to the mother, assuring her that it was quite all right to stay and that the baby's crying was as much a part of the liturgy as everything else. Indeed, he thought to himself, it is this that has enabled the church to grow: the worship of the church has been enabled to hear the cries of the world, and the cries of the world have been made welcome in the church. It hasn't always been easy, but it has borne fruit. The Eucharist was still at the centre of the church's worship. It was also now at the centre of people's lives. And it was changing them.

A CLOSING MEDITATION:
MARY THE EVANGELIST

AT THE BACK OF MANY BIBLES you will find maps plotting the missionary journeys of Paul. They are often thought of as the first missionary journeys of the Church. But this is not the case. The first missionary journey was made by Mary. When she said her yes to God and received the Christ-child, her first response was to go and visit her cousin Elizabeth. Of course, she was bewildered by what was happening and was seeking comfort and help. What could be more natural? But surely her primary motivation was that she wanted to share with someone else the good news that she was experiencing. Mary gives from the overflow of what she has received.[1]

This is a good way of thinking about evangelism. Although only some are called to be evangelists (Ephesians 4:11), all Christians are called to share in the apostolic ministry of witnessing to Jesus by the receiving and sharing of good news. Our witness will be as much through the lives we lead, as the words we say. Mary can help us because she always points beyond herself to Jesus. Do 'whatever he tells you' are her instructions to the servants at the wedding in Cana (John 2:6). 'Behold Jesus', she proclaims in silent witness from her vigil at the cross.

Her example shows us how to respond and be obedient to God. In her encounter with the angel Gabriel we see a pattern of greeting and response which echoes the whole process of evangelism as good news is shared with others and as we, Christ-bearers to the world today, seek out a response. When the angel first tells Mary of God's promise, Luke tells us that she is 'much perplexed' (Luke 1:29). This is the quite normal reaction to a dawning awareness that there might be more to life than we had imagined. Mary was in all probability a faithful Jewish girl, obedient to the promises and prohibitions of her faith and culture. Now she is spun off-centre by the radical intervention of God in her life. The last thing she would have felt like doing is rejoicing! 'How can this be?' she says to the angel (Luke 1:34). Surely this is what most of us have cried out when we first glimpsed the possibility and the purposes of God. We are overwhelmed with astonishment, disbelief, confusion; we are full of searching questions. Faith comes, not through having every question answered, still less every hardship removed – Mary is told that a sword will pierce her heart (Luke 2:35) – but through abandonment to the will of God. Faith comes as a gift in response to our surrender. Freely, though fearfully and tentatively, we say yes to God. This is what is seen in the life of Mary. She places herself at God's disposal. Again and again she points the way to Jesus. Her life is his life; she shares the promise of eternal life with others, because she has received the promise of eternal life from him. 'Let it be to me according to your word' (Luke 1:38) are the words that begin the Christian faith; they are about the free response to God's searching love. Only when we have said these words can evangelism begin. They echo the words of Isaiah: 'Here am I; send me' (Isaiah 6:8). They foreshadow the call of the disciples, who leave everything to follow Jesus.

And so Mary rushes to see her cousin Elizabeth; rushes to tell her good news. The response of the angel to her question – 'How can this be?' – was not so much an answer as a promise: 'The Holy Spirit will come upon you, and the power of the Most High will overshadow you; therefore the child to be born will be holy; he will be called Son of God' (Luke 1:35). Mary is brimming with the Spirit. Through the Holy Spirit Jesus has been formed in her; he takes his flesh from her flesh. This is always the way the Holy Spirit works in the lives of those who believe. We may indeed cry out: how can this be? It seems too amazing that God could make his home in us, but this is the scandalous heart of Christian faith: the God who is everywhere becomes the God who is somewhere. The God who spoke and the universe was, is now a cluster of cells dividing into life in the flood-tide of Mary's womb.

And Elizabeth recognises in Mary this turning of the axis of eternity. It is from this moment that time will be measured. Mary's surrender to the will of God is the pivot of the ages, 'blessed is she who believed that there would be a fulfilment of what was spoken to her by the Lord' (Luke 1:45). Thus it is that as soon as Elizabeth hears Mary's greeting she too is filled with the Holy Spirit and filled with holy joy. So much so that the child in her womb leaps in exultation. It is the first piece of evangelism. Mary bears good news to her cousin. And as the Holy Spirit ignites in Elizabeth's heart, and as the unborn Baptist turns in the womb towards the unborn Christ, so faith comes to life and Mary sings for joy.

What follows – the hymn of praise that we call the Magnificat – is to my mind an evangelistic text. It is a testimony to all that God has done and a proclamation of saving love. This is the God who looks with favour on the lowly; whose faithful love extends across the generations; and whose purposes for the world are those of justice and peace and whose promises are sure.

Apparently, St Augustine said of Mary that she conceived Christ in her heart before she conceived him in her womb. Luke also says that Mary 'treasured in her heart' all the things she knew and experienced (Luke 2:51). Out of the abundance of her heart Mary lives a life of faithful witness to Christ, even though it means her heart will be broken. 'She stands as a model of holiness, obedience, and faith for all Christians.'[2]

The prophet Ezekiel receives the promise from God of a new heart and a new spirit. Furthermore, God promises, 'I will remove from your body the heart of stone and give you a heart of flesh' (Ezekiel 36:26). Although we would love God to remove our heart of stone, for a replacement we would probably choose a bionic, super, never-to-be-hurt sort of heart. But this is not what God offers. He promises a heart of flesh; a heart that will more keenly feel the hurt and confusion of the world; a heart to love; a heart like the heart of God. This is the Christlike love that Mary receives in her heart and it is the love that each of us can receive. Without it there will be no evangelism. This heartfelt love is our motivation, our message and our method.

Sometimes evangelism is seen as either the shallow end of faith – the preserve of the mindlessly enthusiastic – or the macho branch of the church – tub-thumping proclamation and feverish activity. Mary presents another way. Her Magnificat shows that the proclamation of salvation is properly bound up with the proclamation of the kingdom and that the two should not be separated. By her example we learn a contemplative approach to evangelism. She is never afraid to witness to her Son, and does not shrink from the suffering this witness brings, but she is not a preacher, nor a strategist, nor a leader. She is simply the one who, filled with grace and joy, treasures the marvellous works of God in her heart, and from the abundance of her heart lives a life that is translucent of the gospel. The marks of her witness are prayer, testimony, reflection, an abundance of joy and an abandonment to God's will. These are the things we need to foster in our churches so that we may equip Christian people to live Christian lives. What was true for Mary can be true for us. We can be Christ's witnesses today. We can become an evangelising church. Nothing is impossible to God. We do, however, need to say yes to the invitation.

A PRAYER INVITING GOD TO USE US IN THE MINISTRY OF EVANGELISM

Loving God,
make my life a sign of your engaging love:
>   may my heart be penitent,
>   my actions generous,
>   my words be sensitive.

Fill me with longing to share with others the good news I have received,
and anoint my life with your Spirit that Jesus be formed in me:
>   his tongue to speak in me,
>   his hands to work in me,
>   his heart to beat in me.

And so through all I do, and all I am,
>   and with the people where you call me to witness,
>   may Jesus be known
>   and his kingdom established.

RESOURCES

This is inevitably a brief and partial selection of what is available. But I have tried to list not only those resources that come from a specifically catholic standpoint, but also those which will resonate with and challenge catholic parishes wanting to engage with evangelism in the way this book encourages.

Evangelism

Abrahams, William, *The Logic of Evangelism* (Eerdmans, 1996)

Booker, Mike, and Mark Ireland, *Evangelism – which way now? An evaluation of Alpha, Emmaus, Cell church and other contemporary strategies for evangelism* (Church House Publishing, 2003)

Butler, Angela, *Personality and Communicating the Gospel,* Grove Evangelism Series 47 (Grove Books, 1999)

Cottrell, Stephen, *Sacrament, Wholeness and Evangelism,* Grove Evangelism Series 33 (Grove Books, 1996)

Croft, Steven, Yvonne Richmond, and Nick Spencer, *Evangelism in a Spiritual Age: communicating faith in a changing culture* (Church House Publishing, 2005)

Donovan, Vincent J., *Christianity Rediscovered* (Orbis, 1993)

Evangelisation in the Modern World (Catholic Truth Society, 1976)

Finney, John, *Emerging Evangelism* (DLT, 2004)

Fung, Raymond, *The Isaiah Vision* (CCBI, 1992)

Holmes, John, *Vulnerable Evangelism: The Way of Jesus,* Grove Evangelism Series 54 (Grove Books, 2001)

John, Jeffrey (ed.), *Living Evangelism; Affirming Catholicism and Sharing the Faith* (DLT, 1996)

Going for Growth: a strategy for incumbents of smaller parishes in the central and catholic traditions (Affirming Catholicism)

Preparing for Mission Weekends, a leaflet to facilitate evangelism in the local church produced jointly by ReSource, the Oxford diocese and The College of Evangelists, available from ReSource. Their website and the Oxford diocesan website also have evangelism resources available at www.oxford.anglican.org or www.resource-arm.net

Tomlin, Graham, *The Provocative Church* (SPCK, 2004)

Yaconelli, Mark, *Contemplative Youth Ministry* (SPCK, 2006)

Nurture

Ball, Peter, and Malcolm Grundy, *Faith on the Way; A Practical Guide to the Adult Catechumenate* (Continuum, 2000)

Essence; a six–session course for spiritual seekers (Kingsway/CPAS)

John, Jeffrey, *This is our Faith* (Redemptorist Publications, 1995)

See also pp. 56–8 where the nurture courses *Alpha, Emmaus, Faith on the Way* and *Start!* are described.

Apologetics
Harries, Richard, *God outside the box: why spiritual people object to Christianity* (SPCK, 2002)

Prayer
Burnham, Andrew, *Manual* and *Pocket Manual of Anglo-Catholic Devotion*
Cottrell, Stephen, *Praying through life* (Church House Publishing, 2003)
Guiver, George, *Everyday God* (Triangle, 2002)
Nichols, Aidan, *A Spirituality for the Twenty-first Century* (Our Sunday Visitor, 2003)
Warner, Martin, *The Habit of Holiness* (Continuum, 2005)

Church
Jackson, Bob, *Hope for the Church: Contemporary Strategies for Growth* (Church House Publishing, 2002)
 The Road to Growth: Towards a Thriving Church (Church House Publishing, 2005)
Mission-shaped Church: church planting and fresh expressions of church in a changing context, report from a working group of the Church of England's Mission and Public Affairs Council (Church House Publishing, 2004)
Warren, Robert, *The Healthy Churches' Handbook* (Church House Publishing, 2004)

Worship
Conway, Stephen (ed.), *Living the Eucharist* (DLT, 2001)
Earey, Mark, *Liturgical Worship: How it works and why it matters* (Church House Publishing, 2002)
Giles, Richard, *Re-pitching the Tent: re-ordering the church building for worship and mission in the new millennium* (Canterbury Press, 2000)
 Creating Uncommon Worship: transforming the liturgy of the Eucharist (Canterbury Press, 2004)
Marshall, Michael, *Free to Worship: creating transcendent worship today* (Zondervan, 1996)
Perham, Michael, *New handbook of Pastoral Liturgy* (SPCK, 2000)
Ward, Pete (ed.), *Mass Culture: Eucharist and Mission in a Post-Modern World* (Bible Reading Fellowship, 1999)

Books to give to new Christians or for those who want to find out more
Cottrell, Stephen, and Steven Croft, *Travelling Well: A Companion Guide to the Christian Faith* (Church House Publishing, 2000)
Cottrell, Stephen, *On this Rock: Bible Foundations for Christian Living* (Bible Reading Fellowship, 2003)

NOTES

Epigraph
1. *Evangelisation in the Modern World* (Catholic Truth Society, 1976), p. 9.

Introduction
1. I am indebted to Rowan Williams for his 'plotting' of the background to the word mission in his essay 'Doing the Works of God' in *Open to Judgement: Sermons and Addresses* (DLT, 1994).
2. Pope Paul VI, *Evangelisation in the Modern World* (Catholic Truth Society, 1976), p. 38.
3. John Finney, *Emerging Evangelism* (DLT, 2004), p. 28.
4. Robert Farrar Capon, *The Mystery of Christ and why we don't get it* (Wm B. Eerdmans Publishing Co., 2000), p. 9.
5. *ibid.*, p. 115.
6. Donald Elliott, paper written for the Council of Churches for Britain and Ireland Conference for World Mission, quoted in Robert Warren, *Signs of Life* (Church House Publishing, 1996), p. 90.

1: Prayer – the way we access and are renewed by God's vision
1. I have written about this in my book *I Thirst: The Cross – the Great Triumph of Love* (Zondervan, 2003), pp. 131–5.

2: A theological vision: the faith that changes our life and the gospel we share
1. Graham Tomlin has written very powerfully about this aspect of evangelism in his book *The Provocative Church* (SPCK, 2002).
2. Robert Warren, *The Healthy Churches' Handbook* (Church House Publishing, 2004), p. vii.
3. Lesslie Newbigin, *The Gospel in a Pluralist Society* (SPCK, 1989), p. 227.
4. Here I am following closely the notes from the Developing Servant Leaders' Handouts written by Keith Lamdin, Director of the Oxford Diocesan Board of Stewardship, Training, Evangelism and Ministry, DSL Handout Folder, 2004.

3: What kind of church does God want us to be?
1. The Nicene Creed.
2. The report *Mission-shaped Church* (Church House Publishing, 2004, pp. 96–9) also uses these marks as its theological rationale for mission and health.
3. I first argued this in my Grove booklet, *Sacrament, Wholeness and Evangelism* (Grove Books, 1996), pp. 2–5: what we *do* as a church ought to arise out of an understanding of what God has called us to *be*. This in turn was inspired by the book *How to be a Local Church* by John Cole, now sadly out of print. In his influential *Building Missionary Congregations* (Church House Publishing,

1996), Robert Warren used a similar diagram, though he uses the words 'worship', 'community' and 'mission' to describe the three basic vocations of the church.

Intermission: The culture in which we evangelise and the ways we respond

1. Licensing service of a new priest in the Ordinal.
2. Rowan Williams, *Open to Judgement; Sermons and Addresses* (DLT, 1994), pp. 262–3.
3. *ibid.,* p. 262.
4. The Lambeth Commission on Communion, *The Windsor Report* (The Anglican Communion Office, 2004), p. 42.
5. Louis MacNeice, 'Snow', from *Collected Poems* (Faber, 1960).
6. See Lindsay Urwin, 'Of Maypoles and other dances', in *Church Observer* (Winter, 1996), published by the Church Union, pp. 3–6.

4: A model for evangelism

1. See Acts 9.
2. John Finney, *Finding Faith Today: How does it happen?* (Bible Society, 1992).
3. See Luke 24:13ff.
4. See Acts 4:20.
5. This diagram also forms the basis of the *Emmaus* programme of which I am one of the authors and the Mission Weekends programme I worked on with Springboard, the initiative in evangelism of the Archbishops of Canterbury and York.
6. This example, which is developed through the book, is loosely based upon the actual experience of a church in the Diocese of Wakefield, with whom I worked as Missioner in the 1990s.

5: Building a place of nurture

1. Indeed, adoption is the great image that Paul uses to describe the relationship we have with God in Christ (Galatians 4:5 and elsewhere).
2. Research quoted in Mike Booker and Mark Ireland, *Evangelism, which way now? An evaluation of Alpha, Emmaus, Cell church and other contemporary strategies for evangelism* (Church House Publishing, 2003), p. 54.
3. Bob Jackson, *Hope for the Church: contemporary strategies for growth* (Church House Publishing, 2002).
4. Church House Publishing, 1998.
5. See Robert Warren, *The Healthy Churches' Handbook* (Church House Publishing, 2004), p. 42.
6. *The Rule of St Benedict*, trans. Abbot Parry OSB (Gracewing, 1990), p. 83.
7. Jackson, *Hope for the Church for the Church, contemporary strategies for growth*, p. 85.
8. *Common Worship: Christian Initiation* (Church House Publishing, 2006)
9. *Emmaus, the Way of Faith; Stage Two, Nurture* (Church House Publishing, 1996), pp. 108–14.

6: Getting started/Developing contact

1. I am grateful to my old colleague from Springboard, James Lawrence, who not

only first told me this story, but also helped enormously in my understanding of evangelism.

2. Not just anecdotal evidence, nor the heaving shelves of the Mind, Body, Spirit sections of bookshops, but also research such as that undertaken by David Hay and Kate Hunt, *Understanding the Spirituality of People Who Don't Go to Church* (University of Nottingham, 2000).

3. Philip Richter and Leslie J. Francis, *Gone but not Forgotten, Church Leaving and Returning* (DLT, 1998).

7: Conversion

1. Michael Marshall, 'The double grip of glory' in Jeffrey John (ed.), *Living Evangelism* (DLT, 1996), p. 17.

2. *Common Worship, Initiation Services* (Church House Publishing, 1998), p. 22.

3. Henri Nouwen, *The Return of the Prodigal Son* (DLT, 1994), pp. 106–7.

4. For those who are preparing for baptism a confession can be made and the baptism itself can be the absolution.

5. *Common Worship, Services and Prayers for the Church of England, Pastoral Services* (Church House Publishing, 2000), p. 109.

6. Quoted in Robert Atwell, *Celebrating the Saints: Daily Readings for the Calendar of the Church of England* (Canterbury Press, 1998), p. 323.

8: Helping people grow in their faith/Building community

1. The Resources section at the end of the book lists some of the help available in this area of ministry.

2. Nick Page, *The Church Invisible: a journey into the future of the UK Church* (Zondervan, 2004), p. 155.

3. Fr David Garlic developed this model at St Mary's, Lewisham. I'm sure there are others.

4. I am indebted in this section to Steven Croft's thinking and writing on the relationship between evangelism and pastoral care, a much neglected area in church growth theory. In particular see *Ministry in Three Dimensions: Ordination and Leadership 'in' the Local Church* (DLT, 1999), pp. 194–9.

5. Robert Warren, 'Renewing the Church around Spirituality' in *Good News*, Issue 26 (March 1997), p. 7.

9: Evangelising worship

1. Richard Giles, *Creating Uncommon Worship: transforming the liturgy of the Eucharist* (Canterbury Press, 2004), p. 15.

2. Annie Dillard, *Teaching a Stone to Talk: Expeditions and Encounters* (Harper and Row, 1982), quoted in Giles, *Creating Uncommon Worship*, p. 9.

3. Giles, *Creating Uncommon Worship, transforming the liturgy of the Eucharist*, p. 6.

4. Bob Jackson, *The Road to Growth: towards a thriving church* (Church House Publishing, 2005).

5. David Stancliffe, 'Walking in Patterns: Cathedral Worship', in *Flagships of the Spirit: Cathedrals in Society*, edited by Stephen Platten and Christopher Lewis (DLT, 1998), p. 50.

6. Jeffrey John, *Going for Growth: a strategy for incumbents of smaller parishes in*

the central and catholic traditions (Affirming Catholicism), p. 8.

7. *ibid.,* p. 9.

8. Ken Leech, *We Preach Christ Crucified*, (DLT, 1994), p. 14.

9. David Stancliffe, 'Evangelism and Worship' in Jeffrey John (ed.), *Living Evangelism* (DLT, 1996), p. 25.

10. Here I would like to express my great gratitude to Helena del Pino for the way she helped develop this evangelistic ministry through prayer and meditation.

11. Ian Tarrant and Sally Dakin, *Labyrinths and Prayer Stations*, Grove Worship Series 180 (Grove Books Ltd, 2004).

12. Rob Frost, *Essence: A six-session course for today's spiritual seekers* (Kingsway/CPAS).

13. *Mission-shaped Church* (Church House Publishing, 2004).

14. Quoted in John Holmes, *Vulnerable Evangelism*, Grove Evangelism Series 54 (Grove Books, 2001).

15. Pete Ward has been an extremely influential person in this 'movement' and several of his books reflect an exploration of catholic spirituality and worship. In particular *Mass Culture: Eucharist and Mission in a Post-Modern World* (Bible Reading Fellowship, 1999) is a book of essays describing a rediscovery and a creative re-working of Eucharistic worship from the perspective of charismatic evangelicals and through the route of alternative worship. Its very existence says something important about what is happening in the Church.

16. Stephen Cottrell and Tim Sledge, *Vital Statistics*, Springboard.

17. Richard Holloway, 'Introduction' in John (ed.), *Living Evangelism*, p. 5.

18. Quoted in Michael Marshall, *Free to Worship: Creating transcendent worship today* (Marshall Pickering, 1982), p. 1.

19. Quoted in Graham Cray 'The Eucharist and the Post-Modern World' in Ward (ed.), *Mass Culture: Eucharist and Mission in a Post-Modern World*, p. 90.

20. David Stancliffe, 'Evangelism and Worship' in John (ed.), *Living Evangelism*, p. 25.

21. Quoted in *Mission-shaped Church*, p. 13.

22. *Evangelisation in the Modern World* (Catholic Truth Society, 1976), p. 9.

23. William Temple, *Readings in St John's Gospel* (MacMillan and Co, 1939), p. 67.

A closing meditation

1. Much of what follows is taken pretty much verbatim from 'Mary the Evangelist' a chapter I wrote for *Say Yes to God; Mary and the Revealing of the Word Made Flesh*, edited by Martin Warner (Tufton Books, 1999), pp. 47–9. This chapter goes into greater detail about Mary as Evangelist and the Magnificat as an evangelistic text.

2. Agreed Statement of the Anglican and Roman Catholic International Commission, *Mary: Grace and Hope in Christ* (Morehouse Publishing, 2005), p. 48.